BOB DYLAN THE LYRICS 1961—2020

# UNDER THE RED SKY

# 红色天空下

鲍勃 · 迪伦诗歌集 1961—2020

VOL.08

[美]鲍勃·迪伦 著 李皖 译

中信出版集团 | 北京

## 异教徒

*INFIDELS*



附加歌词



## 帝国滑稽剧

*EMPIRE BURLESQUE*

## 哦，慈悲

## *OH MERCY*



## 红色天空下

## *UNDER THE RED SKY*

# *INFIDELS*
# 异教徒



附加歌词

~~They say that oppression is a cruel tutor~~
~~And injustice is a nurse~~
~~You can put your hand in the hand of a man with a nose that can't smell~~
~~But you put your confidence in him and that's worse~~
Snap out of it, baby
People are jealous of you
They smile in your face, but behind your back they hiss
What's a sweetheart like you doin' in a dump like this
YOU KNOW NEWS OF YOU HAS COME DOWN THE LINE EVEN BEFORE YA CAME IN THE DOOR!
THEY SAY IN YOUR FATHER'S HOUSE, THERE'S MANY MANSIONS — EACH ONE OF 'M GOT A FIREPROOF FLOOR!

迪伦走出“基督教三部曲”的专辑取名叫《异教徒》。这个名字是突然蹦进他脑子的，迪伦说并不知道它的意思。但从心理分析的角度来看，这个名字用意曲折但深刻准确。以这张专辑，迪伦从天国俯冲下来，扑向了世俗世界。《异教徒》具有迪伦最积极面对时代变局时所拥有的那种广度，以我之见，它远远超过了历史上他有过的广度。

迪伦的这第22张录音室专辑，诞生于《来一针爱》出版两年后，由哥伦比亚唱片公司于1983年10月27日发行。

《异教徒》的制作团队精英荟萃，有制作人和吉他手马克·诺弗勒（Mark Knopfler），有滚石乐队吉他手米克·泰勒（Mick Taylor），有雷鬼“哼哈二将”斯莱和罗比（Sly & Robbie）。据说，迪伦引进外援的关键原因之一是他对新一轮技术革命产生了理解障碍——当时正值模拟技术向数字技术转变的关口，迪伦对新的数字录音设备玩不转。

迪伦与诺弗勒的合作，既是两类完全不同的艺术家的神交，也隐含着这两者的尖锐冲突。江山易改，本性难移，迪伦还是喜欢快速录音，以抓住藏在音乐生成瞬间的创意。他评论老鹰乐队“歌确实不错，但每个音符都是可以被预测的”。他在《异教徒》里注意到有类似的苗头，立即踩刹车，推倒重来。

马克·诺弗勒有时会为这种合作感到痛苦。他承认塑造迪伦很困难，“我得说，我现在没有以前守规则。不过我觉得，鲍勃作为词作家和诗人，比我更守规则。他绝对是个天才。作为一名歌手——绝对的天才。但要说起音乐，他就普通多了。他的音乐往往只是其诗歌的载体。”

“就吉他和钢琴演奏而言，鲍勃的音乐能力有限，”诺弗勒说，“很初级，但这并不影响他的多样性、旋律感和歌唱。一切都在那里。事实上，他演唱时在钢琴上弹的东西很可爱，尽管很初级。所有这些都证明了一个事实，你不必成为伟大的演奏家。还是那个老故事：如果有些东西是用灵魂演奏的，那才是重要的。”[1]

从这张专辑起，迪伦不再宣扬宗教。在接受《新闻周刊》采访时，他说：“我在音乐中找到了宗教和哲学……我不追随拉比、传教士、传道者，所有那些。我从这些歌曲中学到的比从任何此类宗教实体中学到的都多。”

然而，宗教仍然存在于迪伦的内心，只是现在，它开始观照这个外在世界。开场曲《小丑》指向反基督人物，还提到了过度关注表面世界的民粹主义者（“米开朗琪罗差一点就雕出你的五官”），并且更多注意到了行动而非思想复杂性（“愚人们冲入天使不敢落足之处”）。

《像你这样的甜心》充满了挖苦，其尖刻语气隔十公里都能闻到。它讽刺那些看起来甜的、光鲜的、干净的、美

[1] Heylin, Clinton (1991). *Bob Dylan: Behind the Shades Revisited.* HarperCollins.

的，关键不在女性，有人说所指是教会这类组织，只有表面的体面，却偏离了本质。

《杀人执照》反思所谓“进步”，《工会日薄西山》反省全球化，《和平大使》指向和平主义伪装者，弃用作品《骄傲的脚》警告人类的傲慢。令我觉得惊奇的是，这些作品像是今天写的，迪伦对太空计划、对人类掌控地球的统治力，都持以怀疑和批判，他的眼光仍然有前瞻性。他对全球化的描述放到今天也还是生动的，其中对于资本主义本质的揭示仍然有力，引人深思。《我和我》受启发于当时全球泛非主义拉斯特法里教的一个概念——“上帝存在于每个人身上”，由此探索了迪伦的内在身份和公众形象。时至今日，所有歌曲依然具有新鲜感和启示性，令人深思。

但当时的批评家，包括乐评界最著名的几位，一概认为这些歌曲毫无意义，甚至评价迪伦“变成了一个可恨的疯子”。但只要长耳朵就能听到，这张专辑非同寻常的宽广和深沉、成熟和复杂，具有一般歌曲没有的感染力。在这个方面，它确实很可敬也很讨厌——就像是一篇对世界的檄文，或者说悼词。

《异教徒》于 1983 年 4 月 11 日至 5 月 18 日，在纽约录了 22 场。有 7 首歌曲收入了专辑，同时产生了大批“废品”——也多是杰作。

# JOKERMAN

Standing on the waters casting your bread
While the eyes of the idol with the iron head are glowing
Distant ships sailing into the mist
You were born with a snake in both of your fists while a hurricane
  was blowing
Freedom just around the corner for you
But with the truth so far off, what good will it do?

Jokerman dance to the nightingale tune
Bird fly high by the light of the moon
Oh, oh, oh, Jokerman

So swiftly the sun sets in the sky
You rise up and say goodbye to no one
Fools rush in where angels fear to tread
Both of their futures, so full of dread, you don't show one
Shedding off one more layer of skin
Keeping one step ahead of the persecutor within

Jokerman dance to the nightingale tune

# 小丑[1]

你站在水面撒面包
当铁头圣像两眼放光
远处的船驶入薄雾
你生来两手攥蛇，其时飓风
　鼓荡
自由就在眼前
但真理远在天际，这又有何意义？

小丑随夜莺的鸣啭起舞
小鸟乘月光高高飞起
哦，哦，哦，小丑

天空中的太阳倏忽坠落
你站起身，对着空无一人道别
愚人们冲入天使不敢落足之处
他们这两种未来，都充满恐惧，你一样均未表露
又蜕掉一层皮
比内在的迫害者领先一步

小丑随夜莺的鸣啭起舞

---

[1] 本篇由杨盈盈校译。

Bird fly high by the light of the moon
Oh, oh, oh, Jokerman

You're a man of the mountains, you can walk on the clouds
Manipulator of crowds, you're a dream twister
You're going to Sodom and Gomorrah
But what do you care? Ain't nobody there would want to marry your sister
Friend to the martyr, a friend to the woman of shame
You look into the fiery furnace, see the rich man without any name

Jokerman dance to the nightingale tune
Bird fly high by the light of the moon
Oh, oh, oh, Jokerman

Well, the Book of Leviticus and Deuteronomy
The law of the jungle and the sea are your only teachers
In the smoke of the twilight on a milk-white steed
Michelangelo indeed could've carved out your features
Resting in the fields, far from the turbulent space
Half asleep near the stars with a small dog licking your face

Jokerman dance to the nightingale tune
Bird fly high by the light of the moon
Oh, oh, oh, Jokerman

小鸟乘月光高高飞起
哦，哦，哦，小丑

你是山峦之子，能在云头漫步
是人群操纵者，是梦的龙卷风
将去那所多玛和蛾摩拉城[1]
可是你在乎什么？那儿的人都不愿娶你妹妹
一个殉道者和羞耻妇的朋友
你观察着烈火熔炉，看见了没有名字的财主

小丑随夜莺的鸣啭起舞
小鸟乘月光高高飞起
哦，哦，哦，小丑

哦，《利未记》和《申命记》
丛林和海洋法则是你唯一的老师
黄昏烟雾中，乳白骏马上
米开朗琪罗差一点就雕出你的五官
歇息于田间，远离动荡之地
挨着繁星半眠，小狗轻舔你脸

小丑随夜莺的鸣啭起舞
小鸟乘月光高高飞起
哦，哦，哦，小丑

---

[1] 所多玛和蛾摩拉，两座被上帝毁灭的罪恶之城。

Well, the rifleman's stalking the sick and the lame
Preacherman seeks the same, who'll get there first is uncertain
Nightsticks and water cannons, tear gas, padlocks
Molotov cocktails and rocks behind every curtain
False-hearted judges dying in the webs that they spin
Only a matter of time 'til night comes steppin' in

Jokerman dance to the nightingale tune
Bird fly high by the light of the moon
Oh, oh, oh, Jokerman

It's a shadowy world, skies are slippery grey
A woman just gave birth to a prince today and dressed him in scarlet
He'll put the priest in his pocket, put the blade to the heat
Take the motherless children off the street and place them at the feet of
a harlot
Oh, Jokerman, you know what he wants
Oh, Jokerman, you don't show any response

Jokerman dance to the nightingale tune
Bird fly high by the light of the moon
Oh, oh, oh, Jokerman

噢，步枪手在偷偷靠近病残者
传教士目标相同，谁先到达无法确定
警棍和水枪、催泪瓦斯、挂锁
每一块窗帘后的燃烧弹和石块
假仁假义的法官在自己织就的网里奄奄一息
夜幕降临只是时间问题

小丑随夜莺的鸣啭起舞
小鸟乘月光高高飞起
哦，哦，哦，小丑

这是阴影中的世界，每块天空都是滑溜溜的灰色
今天女人刚生下王子，给他穿上了一身猩红
他将把神父装入口袋，将利刃烧热
带走街头没妈的孩子，放在妓女
　脚边
哦，小丑，你知道他想要什么
哦，小丑，你没有一丝回应

小丑随夜莺的鸣啭起舞
小鸟乘月光高高飞起
哦，哦，哦，小丑

## SWEETHEART LIKE YOU

Well, the pressure's down, the boss ain't here
He gone North, he ain't around
They say that vanity got the best of him
But he sure left here after sundown
By the way, that's a cute hat
And that smile's so hard to resist
But what's a sweetheart like you doin' in a dump like this?

You know, I once knew a woman who looked like you
She wanted a whole man, not just a half
She used to call me sweet daddy when I was only a child
You kind of remind me of her when you laugh
In order to deal in this game, got to make the queen disappear
It's done with a flick of the wrist
What's a sweetheart like you doin' in a dump like this?

You know, a woman like you should be at home
That's where you belong
Watching out for someone who loves you true
Who would never do you wrong
Just how much abuse will you be able to take?
Well, there's no way to tell by that first kiss

## 像你这样的甜心

哦，压力小了，老板走了
他去了北方，不在这儿了
他们说他虚荣心占了上风
但他确实日落后离开了
顺便说一句，那顶帽子真可爱
而那笑容是如此难以抗拒
但是像你这样的甜心，在这样的脏地方干吗？

你知道吧，我以前认识一个长得就像你的女人
她想要一个完整的男人，而不是只一半
她常叫我甜心爹地，那时我还是个孩子
你笑的时候有点儿让我想起她
为了这游戏能玩下去，必须让皇后消失
抖一下手腕就成了
像你这样的甜心，在这样的脏地方干吗？

你知道吧，你这样的女人应该待家里
那才是属于你的地方
留意一个真爱你的人
永远不会错对你
你能忍受多少虐待？
哦，通过初吻是无法判断的

What's a sweetheart like you doin' in a dump like this?

You know you can make a name for yourself
You can hear them tires squeal
You can be known as the most beautiful woman
Who ever crawled across cut glass to make a deal

You know, news of you has come down the line
Even before ya came in the door
They say in your father's house, there's many mansions
Each one of them got a fireproof floor
Snap out of it, baby, people are jealous of you
They smile to your face, but behind your back they hiss
What's a sweetheart like you doin' in a dump like this?

Got to be an important person to be in here, honey
Got to have done some evil deed
Got to have your own harem when you come in the door
Got to play your harp until your lips bleed

They say that patriotism is the last refuge
To which a scoundrel clings
Steal a little and they throw you in jail
Steal a lot and they make you king
There's only one step down from here, baby
It's called the land of permanent bliss
What's a sweetheart like you doin' in a dump like this?

像你这样的甜心，在这样的脏地方干吗？

你知道你会自己扬名
你会听到他们轮胎的尖叫声
爬过雕花玻璃做交易的最美的女人
你会跟她一样出名

你知道吧，你的消息已在传开
甚至在你进门之前
传言说你父亲家中有许多豪宅
每一座都有防火地板
冷静下来，宝贝，人们都嫉妒你
他们面对你微笑，背对你嘲笑
像你这样的甜心，在这样的脏地方干吗？

必须是个重要人物才能在这儿，亲爱的
必须干出一些恶事
进门就得有自己的后宫
必须吹你的口琴，直到嘴唇流血

他们说爱国主义是最后的避难所
无赖会紧紧抓住它
偷得少送你进监狱
偷得多拥你做皇帝
从这里只有一步之遥，宝贝
就是所谓永久极乐之地
像你这样的甜心，在这样的脏地方干吗？

## LICENSE TO KILL

Man thinks 'cause he rules the earth he can do with it as he please
And if things don't change soon, he will
Oh, man has invented his doom
First step was touching the moon

Now, there's a woman on my block
She just sit there as the night grows still
She say who gonna take away his license to kill?

Now, they take him and they teach him and they groom him for life
And they set him on a path where he's bound to get ill
Then they bury him with stars
Sell his body like they do used cars

Now, there's a woman on my block
She just sit there facin' the hill
She say who gonna take away his license to kill?

Now, he's hell-bent for destruction, he's afraid and confused
And his brain has been mismanaged with great skill

## 杀人执照

人认为，因为他统治着地球，所以他可以随心所欲对它
如果情况不很快改变，那么他会
哦，人发明了自己的劫数
第一步是触摸月球[1]

瞧，我的街区有个女人
她就坐那儿，长夜渐寂
她说谁来吊销他的杀人执照？

瞧，他们带走他，教他，终生培养他
引他走上注定毁灭之路
然后用星星把他埋葬
像卖二手车一样卖掉他的身体

瞧，我的街区有个女人
她就坐那儿，面对着山冈
她说谁来吊销他的杀人执照？

瞧，他一心要毁灭，恐惧而迷茫
他的大脑被巧妙地管理不善

---

[1] 第一步是触摸月球，指美国的太空计划。

All he believes are his eyes
And his eyes, they just tell him lies

But there's a woman on my block
Sitting there in a cold chill
She say who gonna take away his license to kill?

Ya may be a noisemaker, spirit maker
Heartbreaker, backbreaker
Leave no stone unturned
May be an actor in a plot
That might be all that you got
'Til your error you clearly learn

Now he worships at an altar of a stagnant pool
And when he sees his reflection, he's fulfilled
Oh, man is opposed to fair play
He wants it all and he wants it his way

Now, there's a woman on my block
She just sit there as the night grows still
She say who gonna take away his license to kill?

他只相信眼睛
而他的眼睛，只告诉他谎言

但我的街区有个女人
坐在那儿，寒意萧瑟
她说谁来吊销他的杀人执照？

你可能是个喧哗者、精神制造师
大魔头、工作狂
想尽千方百计
也可能是剧情中的演员
这或许就是你拥有的全部
直到你清楚意识到你的错误

瞧，他在一潭死水的祭坛礼拜
看到自己的倒影，感到满足
哦，人反对公平竞争
他想要一切，他想要按他的方式

瞧，我的街区有个女人
她就坐那儿，长夜渐寂
她说谁来吊销他的杀人执照？

## MAN OF PEACE

Look out your window, baby, there's a scene you'd like to catch
The band is playing "Dixie," a man got his hand outstretched
Could be the Führer
Could be the local priest
You know sometimes Satan comes as a man of peace

He got a sweet gift of gab, he got a harmonious tongue
He knows every song of love that ever has been sung
Good intentions can be evil
Both hands can be full of grease
You know that sometimes Satan comes as a man of peace

Well, first he's in the background, then he's in the front
Both eyes are looking like they're on a rabbit hunt
Nobody can see through him
No, not even the Chief of Police
You know that sometimes Satan comes as a man of peace

Well, he catch you when you're hoping for a glimpse of the sun
Catch you when your troubles feel like they weigh a ton
He could be standing next to you
The person that you'd notice least

## 和平大使

瞧窗外，宝贝，那儿有个场面值得一看
乐队在弹《迪克西》，一个男人单手平举
可能是“元首”
可能是本地牧师
你知道撒旦有时会装作和平大使

他能说会道，有优美的嗓音
他知晓这世间每支赞美爱的歌曲
善意可能是恶
双手可能沾满油脂
你知道撒旦有时会装作和平大使

哦，一开始在幕后，然后他站到台前
两只眼看似在打兔子
谁都看不穿他
是的，连警察局长也不行
你知道撒旦有时会装作和平大使

哦，他吸住你，当你渴望一缕阳光
吸住你，当你的烦恼有一吨的重量
他可能就站你旁边
是你从不注意的人

I hear that sometimes Satan comes as a man of peace

Well, he can be fascinating, he can be dull
He can ride down Niagara Falls in the barrels of your skull
I can smell something cooking
I can tell there's going to be a feast
You know that sometimes Satan comes as a man of peace

He's a great humanitarian, he's a great philanthropist
He knows just where to touch you, honey, and how you like to be kissed
He'll put both his arms around you
You can feel the tender touch of the beast
You know that sometimes Satan comes as a man of peace

Well, the howling wolf will howl tonight, the king snake will crawl
Trees that've stood for a thousand years suddenly will fall
Wanna get married? Do it now
Tomorrow all activity will cease
You know that sometimes Satan comes as a man of peace

Somewhere Mama's weeping for her blue-eyed boy
She's holding them little white shoes and that little broken toy
And he's following a star
The same one them three men followed from the East
I hear that sometimes Satan comes as a man of peace

我听说撒旦有时会装作和平大使

哦，他可能光彩照人，可能呆滞
可能驾着你的颅骨从尼亚加拉瀑布飞下去
我能闻到做菜香
我敢说正有一场盛宴
你知道撒旦有时会装作和平大使

他是伟大的人道主义者，他是大慈善家
他知道你哪儿敏感，亲爱的，还有你希望被怎样亲吻
他会两手抱定你
你可以感受到野兽温柔的抚摸
你知道撒旦有时会装作和平大使

哦，今夜嚎狼会嚎，王蛇会爬行
屹立千年的树会突然倒下
想结婚吗？现在就结吧
明天一切都将结束
你知道撒旦有时会装作和平大使

有一个地方，妈妈为她的蓝眼睛儿子哭泣
她抱着小白鞋和破碎的小玩具
而他在追一颗星
那三人从东方追随的那颗星
我听说撒旦有时会装作和平大使

## UNION SUNDOWN

Well, my shoes, they come from Singapore
My flashlight's from Taiwan
My tablecloth's from Malaysia
My belt buckle's from the Amazon
You know, this shirt I wear comes from the Philippines
And the car I drive is a Chevrolet
It was put together down in Argentina
By a guy makin' thirty cents a day

Well, it's sundown on the union
And what's made in the U.S.A.
Sure was a good idea
'Til greed got in the way

Well, this silk dress is from Hong Kong
And the pearls are from Japan
Well, the dog collar's from India
And the flower pot's from Pakistan
All the furniture, it says "Made in Brazil"
Where a woman, she slaved for sure
Bringin' home thirty cents a day to a family of twelve
You know, that's a lot of money to her

## 工会日薄西山

哦，我的鞋子来自新加坡
我的手电筒来自台湾
我的桌布来自马来西亚
我的皮带扣来自亚马逊
你知道吧，我身上这件衬衫来自菲律宾
我开的车是雪佛兰
是阿根廷组装的
装它的伙计每天挣三十美分

哦，工会日薄西山
还包括美国制造
这当然是个好主意
直到贪婪挡了道

哦，这件真丝裙来自香港
珍珠来自日本
哦，狗项圈来自印度
花盆来自巴基斯坦
所有的家具，标注着“巴西制造”
那边有个女人，肯定玩儿命干
每天给一家十二口带回三十美分
你知道，这对她来说是一大笔钱

Well, it's sundown on the union
And what's made in the U.S.A.
Sure was a good idea
'Til greed got in the way

Well, you know, lots of people complainin' that there is no work
I say, "Why you say that for
When nothin' you got is U.S.–made?"
They don't make nothin' here no more
You know, capitalism is above the law
It say, "It don't count 'less it sells"
When it costs too much to build it at home
You just build it cheaper someplace else

Well, it's sundown on the union
And what's made in the U.S.A.
Sure was a good idea
'Til greed got in the way

Well, the job that you used to have
They gave it to somebody down in El Salvador
The unions are big business, friend
And they're goin' out like a dinosaur
They used to grow food in Kansas
Now they want to grow it on the moon and eat it raw

哦，工会日薄西山
还包括美国制造
这当然是个好主意
直到贪婪挡了道

哦，你知道，很多人都抱怨没工作
我说：“干吗还说这个
当你买到的已没一样是美国造？”
他们什么都不在这儿做了
你知道，资本主义高于法律
上写：“除非能卖，否则不作数”
当国内制造成本太高
你就会找更便宜的地方生产

哦，工会日薄西山
还包括美国制造
这当然是个好主意
直到贪婪挡了道

哦，你一度拥有的那份儿工
他们给了萨尔瓦多的一个人
工会是个大机构，朋友
他们会像恐龙一样走出去
他们过去在堪萨斯种粮
现在想到月亮上种并生吃

I can see the day coming when even your home garden
Is gonna be against the law

Well, it's sundown on the union
And what's made in the U.S.A.
Sure was a good idea
'Til greed got in the way

Democracy don't rule the world
You'd better get that in your head
This world is ruled by violence
But I guess that's better left unsaid
From Broadway to the Milky Way
That's a lot of territory indeed
And a man's gonna do what he has to do
When he's got a hungry mouth to feed

Well, it's sundown on the union
And what's made in the U.S.A.
Sure was a good idea
'Til greed got in the way

我可以预见那一天，甚至你家的花园
到时都会触犯法律

哦，工会日薄西山
还包括美国制造
这当然是个好主意
直到贪婪挡了道

民主不统治世界
你最好记住了
这世界由暴力统治
但我想还是不说为好
从百老汇到银河系
确实是很大一片版图
一个人必然会如此
当他有一张填不满的大嘴

哦，工会日薄西山
还包括美国制造
这当然是个好主意
直到贪婪挡了道

# I AND I

Been so long since a strange woman has slept in my bed
Look how sweet she sleeps, how free must be her dreams
In another lifetime she must have owned the world, or been faithfully wed
To some righteous king who wrote psalms beside moonlit streams

I and I
In creation where one's nature neither honors nor forgives
I and I
One says to the other, no man sees my face and lives

Think I'll go out and go for a walk
Not much happenin' here, nothin' ever does
Besides, if she wakes up now, she'll just want me to talk
I got nothin' to say, 'specially about whatever was

I and I
In creation where one's nature neither honors nor forgives
I and I
One says to the other, no man sees my face and lives

Took an untrodden path once, where the swift don't win the race
It goes to the worthy, who can divide the word of truth

## 我和我

已经很久了没有陌生女睡我床上
看她睡得多香，她的梦应该无比自由
在另一世她定然拥有世界，或忠贞地嫁予
月下溪旁作着赞美诗的某位正义君主

我和我
生来天性中既无尊崇亦无宽恕
我和我
一个对另一个说，人见我面不得活

我想我该走出去，散散步
这儿无事发生，什么事也不会有
再说，若是她醒了，她也只是想听我说话
我无话可说，尤其是讲以前的事

我和我
生来天性中既无尊崇亦无宽恕
我和我
一个对另一个说，人见我面不得活

曾走过一条无人涉足的小径，在那儿快跑的不能赢
胜利属于能分解真理的圣者

Took a stranger to teach me, to look into justice's beautiful face
And to see an eye for an eye and a tooth for a tooth

I and I
In creation where one's nature neither honors nor forgives
I and I
One says to the other, no man sees my face and lives

Outside of two men on a train platform there's nobody in sight
They're waiting for spring to come, smoking down the track
The world could come to an end tonight, but that's all right
She should still be there sleepin' when I get back

I and I
In creation where one's nature neither honors nor forgives
I and I
One says to the other, no man sees my face and lives

Noontime, and I'm still pushin' myself along the road, the darkest part
Into the narrow lanes, I can't stumble or stay put
Someone else is speakin' with my mouth, but I'm listening only to my heart
I've made shoes for everyone, even you, while I still go barefoot

I and I
In creation where one's nature neither honors nor forgives
I and I
One says to the other, no man sees my face and lives

他带了个异乡人教我，看清正义的美丽面目
也看明白以眼还眼，以牙还牙

我和我
生来天性中既无尊崇亦无宽恕
我和我
一个对另一个说，人见我面不得活

除了火车月台上的两人，看不见有别人
他们在等春天来临，沿着铁轨抽烟
可能今晚世界就会毁灭，但这没什么
她应该还在睡，当我回到家里

我和我
生来天性中既无尊崇亦无宽恕
我和我
一个对另一个说，人见我面不得活

正午了，我仍逼自己走在路上，这最黑的一段
进入这窄巷，我无法踉跄前行也不能留在原处
有人用我的嘴说话，但我只听从自己的心
我给每人都做了鞋，包括你，而我自己仍赤着双足

我和我
生来天性中既无尊崇亦无宽恕
我和我
一个对另一个说，人见我面不得活

## DON'T FALL APART ON ME TONIGHT

Just a minute before you leave, girl
Just a minute before you touch the door
What is it that you're trying to achieve, girl?
Do you think we can talk about it some more?
You know, the streets are filled with vipers
Who've lost all ray of hope
You know, it ain't even safe no more
In the palace of the Pope

Don't fall apart on me tonight
I just don't think that I could handle it
Don't fall apart on me tonight
Yesterday's just a memory
Tomorrow is never what it's supposed to be
And I need you, yeah

Come over here from over there, girl
Sit down here. You can have my chair

# 今夜别崩溃[1]

等一分钟再走，姑娘
等一分钟再去开门
你想要达成什么，姑娘？
你觉得我们能再谈谈吗？
你知道，现在街上到处是毒蛇
它们失去了全部希望
你知道，就连教皇的宫殿
如今都不再安全[2]

今夜别崩溃
我怕我无法应对
今夜别崩溃
昨日不过是记忆
明日永不如预期
而我需要你，是的

过来吧，姑娘
坐这儿来。你可以坐我的位子

---

[1] 本篇由杨盈盈校译。

[2] 1981 年 5 月 13 日，罗马天主教宗若望·保禄二世在梵蒂冈圣伯多禄广场准备演讲时遭到枪击。

I can't see us goin' anywhere, girl
The only place open is a thousand miles away and I can't take you there
I wish I'd have been a doctor
Maybe I'd have saved some life that had been lost
Maybe I'd have done some good in the world
'Stead of burning every bridge I crossed

Don't fall apart on me tonight
I just don't think that I could handle it
Don't fall apart on me tonight
Yesterday's just a memory
Tomorrow is never what it's supposed to be
And I need you, oh, yeah

I ain't too good at conversation, girl
So you might not know exactly how I feel
But if I could, I'd bring you to the mountaintop, girl
And build you a house made out of stainless steel
But it's like I'm stuck inside a painting
That's hanging in the Louvre
My throat start to tickle and my nose itches
But I know that I can't move

Don't fall apart on me tonight
I just don't think that I could handle it
Don't fall apart on me tonight

我不知道我们能去哪儿，姑娘
唯一还开着的地方在千里外，我无法带你去
多希望我是医生
也许就能救回几条命
也许就能在这世间做几件好事
而不是去烧掉我走过的每座桥

今夜别崩溃
我怕我无法应对
今夜别崩溃
昨日不过是记忆
明日永不如预期
而我需要你，哦，是的

我不太善于言辞，姑娘
所以你可能不很明白我的感受
但如果可以，我会带你到山顶，姑娘
给你造一座不锈钢的房子
然而我就像困进了一幅画
挂在卢浮宫
我的喉咙难受，鼻子发痒
但我知道我不能动

今夜别崩溃
我怕我无法应对
今夜别崩溃

Yesterday's gone but the past lives on
Tomorrow's just one step beyond
And I need you, oh, yeah

Who are these people who are walking towards you?
Do you know them or will there be a fight?
With their humorless smiles so easy to see through
Can they tell you what's wrong from what's right?
Do you remember St. James Street
Where you blew Jackie P.'s mind?
You were so fine, Clark Gable would have fell at your feet
And laid his life on the line

Let's try to get beneath the surface waste, girl
No more booby traps and bombs
No more decadence and charm
No more affection that's misplaced, girl
No more mudcake creatures lying in your arms
What about that millionaire with the drumsticks in his pants?
He looked so baffled and so bewildered
When he played and we didn't dance

Don't fall apart on me tonight
I just don't think that I could handle it

昨日已逝，但往昔永存
明日只差一步
而我需要你，哦，是的

那些朝你走去的人是谁？
你认识他们，还是会有一场争吵？
他们毫无幽默感的笑那么容易识破
他们能告诉你什么对什么错吗？
你还记得圣詹姆斯街吗
在那里你让杰基·P 昏头奋脑？
你多么妙啊，克拉克·盖博[1]也会舍命一搏
在你脚下拜倒

让我们试着进入表层以下吧，姑娘
不再有陷阱和炸弹
不再有颓废和蛊惑
不再有错位的爱慕，姑娘
不再有泥饼生物躺在你的怀里
那个裤子里有鼓槌的百万富翁呢？
他看起来多困惑，多无措
当他在演奏而我们却并不跳舞

今夜别崩溃
我怕我无法应对

[1] 克拉克·盖博，美国电影明星，《乱世佳人》男主角。

Don't fall apart on me tonight

Yesterday's just a memory

Tomorrow is never what it's supposed to be

And I need you, yeah

今夜别崩溃
昨日不过是记忆
明日永不如预期
而我需要你，是的

## BLIND WILLIE MCTELL

Seen the arrow on the doorpost
Saying, "This land is condemned
All the way from New Orleans
To new Jerusalem"
I traveled through East Texas
Where many martyrs fell
And I can tell you one thing
Nobody can sing the blues
Like Blind Willie McTell

Well, I heard that hoot owl singing
As they were taking down the tents
The stars above the barren trees
Were his only audience
Them charcoal gypsy maidens
Can strut their feathers well
And I can tell you one thing
Nobody can sing the blues
Like Blind Willie McTell

## 盲人威利·麦克泰尔[1]

看那门柱上的箭
写着："这土地已被诅咒
从新奥尔良
到新耶路撒冷"
我走遍得克萨斯东
许多殉道者死在这里
我可以告诉你一件事
没人能把蓝调唱得
像盲人威利·麦克泰尔那样

哦，我听见猫头鹰在唱
当他们拆掉帐篷
裸树上的星星
是他唯一的听众
皮肤黝黑的吉卜赛女郎
把羽毛炫得漂亮
我可以告诉你一件事
没人能把蓝调唱得
像盲人威利·麦克泰尔那样

---

[1] 盲人威利·麦克泰尔（1898—1959），黑人布鲁斯歌手、吉他手，演奏和演唱柔和雅致，具有宗教歌曲的崇高圣洁感。

There's a woman by the river
With some fine young handsome man
He's dressed up like a squire
Bootlegged whiskey in his hand
Some of them died in the battle
Some of them survived as well
And I can tell you one thing
Nobody can sing the blues
Like Blind Willie McTell

Well, God is in His heaven
And we all want what's His
But power and greed and corruptible seed
Seem to be all that there is
I'm gazing out the window
Of the St. James Hotel
And I can tell you one thing
Nobody can sing the blues
Like Blind Willie McTell

河边有个女人
和俊小伙儿在一起
小伙儿身披盛装像乡绅
手上端着私酿威士忌
他们有些人战死沙场
有些人活了下来
我可以告诉你一件事
没人能把蓝调唱得
像盲人威利·麦克泰尔那样

哦，上帝身在天堂
我们都想要他的奖赏
但是权力、贪欲和腐败种子
似乎成了这儿的一切
我在圣詹姆斯旅馆
透过窗户向外望
我可以告诉你一件事
没人能把蓝调唱得
像盲人威利·麦克泰尔那样

## FOOT OF PRIDE

Like the lion tears the flesh off of a man
So can a woman who passes herself off as a male
They sang "Danny Boy" at his funeral and the Lord's Prayer
Preacher talking 'bout Christ betrayed
It's like the earth just opened and swallowed him up
He reached too high, was thrown back to the ground
You know what they say about bein' nice to the right people on the way up
Sooner or later you gonna meet them comin' down

Well, there ain't no goin' back
When your foot of pride come down
Ain't no goin' back

Hear ya got a brother named James, don't forget faces or names
Sunken cheeks and his blood is mixed
He looked straight into the sun and said revenge is mine
But he drinks, and drinks can be fixed
Sing me one more song, about ya love me to the moon and the stranger
And your fall-by-the sword love affair with Errol Flynn
In these times of compassion when conformity's in fashion
Say one more stupid thing to me before the final nail is driven in

## 骄傲的脚

就像狮子撕下人的肉
冒充男性的女人也会这样
他们在他的葬礼上唱《少年丹尼》和《主祷文》
牧师说起基督被出卖的事
就像大地开口将他吞没
他爬得太高，被扔回地上
你知道吧，他们说向上爬时你要对好人好点
因为迟早你掉下来，你们还会遇上

哦，没有回头路
当你骄傲的脚踏下去
没有回头路

听说你有个兄弟叫詹姆斯，别忘记面孔和名字
他脸颊深陷是混血儿
直视着太阳说申冤在我
然而他喝酒，而酒会被动手脚
再给我唱首歌吧，唱你爱我像月亮像那陌生人
唱你和埃罗尔·弗林倒在刀下的风流韵事
这充满同情心的时代，从众成了时尚
再给我讲件蠢事吧，趁最后一根钉还没钉进去

Well, there ain't no goin' back
When your foot of pride come down
Ain't no goin' back

There's a retired businessman named Red
Cast down from heaven and he's out of his head
He feeds off of everyone that he can touch
He said he only deals in cash or sells tickets to a plane crash
He's not somebody that you play around with much
Miss Delilah is his, a Phillistine is what she is
She'll do wondrous works with your fate, feed you coconut
bread, spice buns in your bed
If you don't mind sleepin' with your head face down in a grave

Well, there ain't no goin' back
When your foot of pride come down
Ain't no goin' back

Well, they'll choose a man for you to meet tonight
You'll play the fool and learn how to walk through doors
How to enter into the gates of paradise
No, how to carry a burden too heavy to be yours

哦，没有回头路
当你骄傲的脚踏下去
没有回头路

有一个退休商人名叫雷德[1]
被从天上抛下来，他疯了
他榨取每一个他能接触的人
说他只收现金，只卖失事飞机的机票
他不是你常混一起的人
大利拉[2]小姐是他的人，她就是一市侩
会用匪夷所思的事给你转运，在床上喂你椰子面包、
　香料点心
如果你不介意在墓地里脸朝下睡觉

哦，没有回头路
当你骄傲的脚踏下去
没有回头路

哦，今夜他们会挑个人与你会面
你会出洋相，学着如何穿过一道道关
如何进入天堂大门
不，是如何挑起对你太重的重担

---

[1] 雷德（Red），暗指撒旦，基督教中红色代表血、罪、死亡，是上帝用来表示撒旦的颜色，比如大红龙。《圣经》中撒旦被逐出天堂。

[2] 大利拉，参孙情妇，出卖参孙，是非利士人。

Yeah, from the stage they'll be tryin' to get water outa rocks
A whore will pass the hat, collect a hundred grand and say
thanks
They like to take all this money from sin, build big universities
to study in
Sing "Amazing Grace" all the way to the Swiss banks

Well, there ain't no goin' back
When your foot of pride come down
Ain't no goin' back

They got some beautiful people out there, man
They can be a terror to your mind and show you how to hold
your tongue
They got mystery written all over their forehead
They kill babies in the crib and say only the good die young
They don't believe in mercy
Judgement on them is something that you'll never see
They can exalt you up or bring you down main route
Turn you into anything that they want you to be

Well, there ain't no goin' back
When your foot of pride come down
Ain't no goin' back

是啊，舞台上他们将尝试从磐石取水[1]
一个妓女将递来帽子，募集十万美金再说声
　谢谢
他们想拿这些取自罪孽的钱，建起供人学习的
　超级大学
一路唱着《天恩浩荡》去瑞士银行

哦，没有回头路
当你骄傲的脚踏下去
没有回头路

他们那儿有一些漂亮的人，老弟
他们会让你心生惶恐，教你如何
　管住嘴
他们的前额上写满了神秘
他们杀掉婴儿床上的婴儿，说只有好人才会早死
他们不相信仁慈
他们受到的报应是你永远看不见的
他们会把你捧上天或把你砸下地
把你变成他们想成就的玩意儿

哦，没有回头路
当你骄傲的脚踏下去
没有回头路

---

[1] 《圣经》中摩西曾两次杖击磐石出水。

Yes, I guess I loved him too
I can still see him in my mind climbin' that hill
Did he make it to the top, well he probably did and dropped
Struck down by the strength of the will
Ain't nothin' left here partner, just the dust of a plague that has
left this whole town afraid
From now on, this'll be where you're from
Let the dead bury the dead. Your time will come
Let hot iron blow as he raised the shade

Well, there ain't no goin' back
When your foot of pride come down
Ain't no goin' back

是的，我想我也爱他
脑海中我还能看到他爬那座山
他爬到顶了吗，哦他可能到了又掉下去了
被意志的力量击溃
这儿什么都没了伙计，除了让全镇恐惧的
　瘟疫之尘
从今往后，这儿就是你的家乡
就让死人埋死人。你的时辰将至
就让热铁爆炸，当他唤来了鬼魂

哦，没有回头路
当你骄傲的脚踏下去
没有回头路

## LORD PROTECT MY CHILD

For his age, he's wise
He's got his mother's eyes
There's gladness in his heart
He's young and he's wild
My only prayer is, if I can't be there
Lord, protect my child

As his youth now unfolds
He is centuries old
Just to see him at play makes me smile
No matter what happens to me
No matter what my destiny
Lord, protect my child

The whole world is asleep
You can look at it and weep
Few things you find are worthwhile
And though I don't ask for much
No material things to touch
Lord, protect my child

He's young and on fire

## 主啊，保护我的孩子

以他的年纪，他很聪明
有他母亲的眼睛
内心充满喜悦
他年少，他狂野
我唯一的祈祷是，若我不能在那儿
主啊，保护我的孩子

随着青春的展开
他历经了数个世纪
只是看他玩耍，我都会微笑
不管我遭遇什么
不管我命运如何
主啊，保护我的孩子

全世界都在沉睡
你可以望着它垂泪
你找到的很少值得
尽管我要的不多
有形万物皆不可触
主啊，保护我的孩子

他年轻气盛

Full of hope and desire
In a world that's been raped and defiled
If I fall along the way
And can't see another day
Lord, protect my child

There'll be a time I hear tell
When all will be well
When God and man will be reconciled
But until men lose their chains
And righteousness reigns
Lord, protect my child

充满希望焦渴
在一个被蹂躏玷污的世界
如果我倒在路上
再也见不到明天
主啊，保护我的孩子

我听说终有一日
一切都会好起来
上帝将与人和解
但在人们失去锁链
而公义掌权之前
主啊，保护我的孩子

## SOMEONE'S GOT A HOLD OF MY HEART
(EARLY VERSION OF "TIGHT CONNECTION TO MY HEART")

They say, "Eat, drink and be merry"
"Take the bull by the horns"
I keep seeing visions of you, a lily among thorns
Everything looks a little far away to me

Gettin' harder and harder to recognize the trap
Too much information about nothin'
Too much educated rap
It's just like you told me, just like you said it would be

The moon rising like wildfire
I feel the breath of a storm
Something I got to do tonight
You go inside and stay warm

Someone's got a hold of my heart
Someone's got a hold of my heart
Someone's got a hold of my heart
You—
Yeah, you got a hold of my heart

## 有人抓住了我的心

（《与我的心密切相关》早期版本）

人们说："吃喝玩乐"
"斗牛抓角"
我不停看见你的幻象，荆棘中一朵百合
一切都像有一点遥不可及

越来越难认出陷阱
太多毫无意义的信息
太多有教养的闲扯
就像你告诉我的，就像你曾经预见的

月亮野火般升起
我感觉到暴风雨的气息
今晚我得去办点事
你进去，别冻着

有人抓住了我的心
有人抓住了我的心
有人抓住了我的心
你——
是啊，你抓住了我的心

Just got back from a city of flaming red skies
Everybody thinks with their stomach
There's plenty of spies
Every street is crooked, they just wind around till they disappear

Madame Butterfly, she lulled me to sleep
Like an ancient river
So wide and deep
She said, "Be easy, baby, ain't nothin' worth stealin' here"

You're the one I've been waitin' for
You're the one I desire
But you must first realize
I'm not another man for hire

Someone's got a hold of my heart
Someone's got a hold of my heart
Someone's got a hold of my heart
You, you, you, you
Yeah, you got a hold of my heart

Hear that hot-blooded singer
On the bandstand croon
September song, Memphis in June
While they're beating the devil out of a guy who's wearing
 a powder blue wig

刚从一座天空火红的城市回来
人人用胃在思考
密探多极了
条条街曲曲弯弯，绕来绕去直到消失不见

蝴蝶夫人，她哄我睡觉
像一条古老的河
如此宽阔深杳
她说："放松孩子，这儿没什么值得偷的"

你是我一直在等的人
你是我渴望的人
但你必须先明白
我并不是又一个可供雇用的男人

有人抓住了我的心
有人抓住了我的心
有人抓住了我的心
你、你、你、你
是啊，你抓住了我的心

听那个热血歌手
在露天舞台上低吟
九月之歌，《六月的孟菲斯》
这时他们在暴打一个戴淡蓝
　假发的人

I been to Babylon

I gotta confess

I could still hear the voice crying in the wilderness

What looks large from a distance, close up is never that big

Never could learn to drink that blood and call it wine

Never could learn to look at your face and call it mine

Someone's got a hold of my heart

Someone's got a hold of my heart

Someone's got a hold of my heart

You—

Yeah, you got a hold of my heart

我去过巴比伦
我必须承认
我依然能听见旷野里的呼喊声
远看很大，近看却并非如此
永远学不会饮血，还把它叫作酒
永远学不会看着你的脸，说你是我的

有人抓住了我的心
有人抓住了我的心
有人抓住了我的心
你——
是啊，你抓住了我的心

## TELL ME

Tell me—I've got to know
Tell me—Tell me before I go
Does that flame still burn, does that fire still glow
Or has it died out and melted like the snow
Tell me
Tell me

Tell me—what are you focused upon
Tell me—will it come to me after you're gone
Tell me quick with a glance on the side
Shall I hold you close or shall I let you go by
Tell me
Tell me

Are you lookin' at me and thinking of somebody else
Can you feel the heat and the beat of my pulse
Do you have any secrets
That will only come out in time
Do you lay in bed and stare at the stars
Is your main friend someone who's an old acquaintance of ours
Tell me
Tell me

## 告诉我吧

告诉我吧——我得知道
告诉我吧——我走之前告诉我
那火焰还在烧吗，那火还在亮吗
还是已经熄灭，像雪一样化了
告诉我吧
告诉我吧

告诉我吧——你在关注什么
告诉我吧——你走后我会意识到吗
赶紧递个眼色告诉我
我是该将你抱紧还是任你走过
告诉我吧
告诉我吧

你看着我却想着别人吗
你能感觉到我脉搏的热力和跳动吗
你有什么秘密
到时候就会揭开吗
你躺在床上瞪着星星吗
你的主要朋友都是我们的老相识吗
告诉我吧
告诉我吧

Tell me—what's in back of them pretty brown eyes
Tell me—behind what door your treasure lies
Ever gone broke in a big way
Ever done the opposite of what the experts say
Tell me
Tell me

Is it some kind of game that you're playin' with me
Am I imagining something that never can be
Do you have any morals
Do you have any point of view
Is that a smile I see on your face
Will it take you to glory or to disgrace
Tell me
Tell me

Tell me—is my name in your book
Tell me—will you go back and take another look
Tell me the truth, tell me no lies
Are you someone whom anyone prays for or cries
Tell me
Tell me

告诉我吧——那漂亮的棕色眼睛后面有什么
告诉我吧——你的金银财宝藏在哪扇门后
你不可收拾地破产过？
和专家说的背道而驰？
告诉我吧
告诉我吧

你是在和我玩什么游戏吗
我是在想象不可能发生的事吗
你有道德观吗
你有任何观点吗
我在你脸上看到的是笑容吗
它将带给你荣耀还是耻辱呢
告诉我吧
告诉我吧

告诉我吧——我的名字在你书里吗
告诉我吧——你会回去再看一眼吗
告诉我真相，别撒谎
你是人们要祈祷和哭泣的人吗
告诉我吧
告诉我吧

## *EMPIRE BURLESQUE*
## 帝国滑稽剧

与我的心密切相关（有人见到我的爱人吗）

终于看见真的你

我会记得你

干干净净的孩子

永远不一样了

信你自己

充满感情的，你的

当黑夜从天空落下

什么东西着了，宝贝

黑暗的眼睛

(hesitated)
If I'd a thought about, I wouldn't've done it, I think I
would a let it slide
If I'd a lived my life by what others think, the heart
inside me would've died
But I ... for man's ..... cheap morality
Some one had to reach for the rising star, it looked like it
was up to me

《帝国滑稽剧》出版于 1985 年 6 月 10 日，是迪伦第 23 张录音室专辑。

此时，迪斯科音乐（disco）和迈克尔·杰克逊（Michael Jackson）风行全球，甚至中国的年轻人也在跳太空步和机器舞。迪伦在该专辑制作期间，抽空参加了 40 位美国歌星联唱的《我们就是世界》（“We Are the World”）的录制，这首歌作为欧美乐坛应对非洲饥荒进行的“拯救生命”行动的一环，风靡全球。次年，中国百名歌手奉献了他们的联唱《让世界充满爱》，在“首都体育馆”同一台演唱会上，《一无所有》和中国摇滚诞生。

这是冷战阴云飘散的年代，是全球化打开大门的年代，是世界做着“天下一家”大梦的年代。迪伦把他的新专辑命名为《帝国滑稽剧》，显然对此有所感应，这个“帝国”当然暗指美国。

《帝国滑稽剧》中几乎没有政治歌曲，除了《干干净净的孩子》。这首“迄今最尖锐的越战老兵之歌”（罗伯特·克里斯戈语）并不关涉当下，讲的是美国的政治旧债，但歌词中“他买了美国梦，可这让他负债累累”这句话，引发了长久的议论。

在娱乐指数猛升，世界洋溢着一片爱的气息的氛围下，迪伦把《帝国滑稽剧》的混音制作交给了阿瑟·贝克（Arthur Baker）——现代舞曲的炼金术士。在贝克处理下，这张专辑染上了明显的20世纪80年代“流行风”，一股时尚金属质感的酷意。专辑受到摇滚乐迷和摇滚批评家的差评，认为它失去了迪伦的特色。

有评论称其为“迪斯科迪伦”“平庸的流行歌曲”，也有报道说迪伦试图创造一种“当代音响”。迪伦带点儿玩笑地回应说，他对新音乐一无所知，他仍然在听查理·帕顿（Charley Patton）——密西西比三角洲古老的布鲁斯歌曲。

专辑有一部分歌词引起了评论界的浓厚兴趣，对其奇特的灵感来源多有考据和挖掘。《与我的心密切相关（有人见到我的爱人吗）》《终于看见真的你》《我会记得你》《永远不一样了》《当黑夜从天空落下》这些歌词仿佛重回好莱坞的黄金年代，像是20世纪40—60年代电影的对白拼贴，也拼贴进了科幻电视剧集《星际迷航》的台词。

这些歌词形成了关联密切、整体统一的词风，构成了整张专辑的基础风格。它们都属于情歌，事关两性间的磕磕绊绊，非常口语化，不乏琐碎，但是琐碎中意涵丰富，上下句间句意跳跃大，感情真挚强烈，其语言风格、美学面貌在诗史上少有。

《信你自己》是迪伦的道德书，直白而坚决，将“信自己”立于信的原点，表明他虽然是个信徒，却是个彻底的自由主义分子，在信仰上不依靠他人，当然，也不依靠教会。迪伦直白表明自己思想主张的歌，只有这一首。勉强可算作这类的，顶多还可加上20世纪60年代的《这不是我，宝贝》《我真正想做的事》——但这两首都是情歌，仅表达爱情观念。

《充满感情的，你的》形式上很别致，篇幅很短，但句子很长，像是由一束情书集成。《什么东西着了，宝贝》用意不寻常，显见企图心大，与《当黑夜从天空落下》一样，是借用情话对现状及未来有所预言的作品，直到录制的一刻迪伦还在不断修改。《圣经》末日情结还在影响他，歌词像是噩兆，显示了他满腹的怀疑和不祥的预感。

《黑暗的眼睛》是词语密集的意象短诗，也是全部使用长句，具有与典型迪伦风格不同的样貌。它是因临时需要急就的终曲，触发它的是迪伦在午夜走廊遇见的应召女郎。“她有一种美丽，但它不适合这个世界。可怜的人儿，她注定要在这个走廊里走上一千年。”在自传中，迪伦这样写道。

从创作经过看，这张专辑经历了特别长的过程，特别多的事情干扰，特别大的人员变动，特别频繁的作品更改、废弃、重来、再造。此时，迪伦在创作上有一个较大变化：零星录音成为常态。这导致这张专辑从 1984 年 7 月 26 日一直折腾到 1985 年 3 月 23 日，用了不下 5 家录音室，进行了 40 多次录音，请了 28 位音乐人（包括 5 位伴唱歌手、8 位吉他手、4 位贝斯手、4 位键盘手、1 位萨克斯手、1 位打击乐手和 5 位鼓手），才终于完成。

# TIGHT CONNECTION TO MY HEART (HAS ANYBODY SEEN MY LOVE)

Well, I had to move fast
And I couldn't with you around my neck
I said I'd send for you and I did
What did you expect?
My hands are sweating
And we haven't even started yet
I'll go along with the charade
Until I can think my way out
I know it was all a big joke
Whatever it was about
Someday maybe
I'll remember to forget

I'm gonna get my coat
I feel the breath of a storm
There's something I've got to do tonight
You go inside and stay warm

## 与我的心密切相关
## （有人见到我的爱人吗）[1]

唉，我得赶紧走了
你搂着我脖子可不行
我说过我会派人接你并且做到了
你还指望什么？
我的手在出汗
可我们还什么都没干
我顺着这样装装样子
直到我能想到出路
我知道这完全是个大笑话
不管它到底咋回事
也许有一天
我会记得忘记

要去拿我的外套
我感觉到暴风雨的气息
今晚我得去办点事
你进去，别冻着

---

[1] 本首歌词多处源自电影台词，尤其是亨弗莱·鲍嘉主演的电影中的台词。本首及这一辑的所有歌词，均由郝佳校译。

Has anybody seen my love
Has anybody seen my love
Has anybody seen my love
I don't know
Has anybody seen my love?

You want to talk to me
Go ahead and talk
Whatever you got to say to me
Won't come as any shock
I must be guilty of something
You just whisper it into my ear
Madame Butterfly
She lulled me to sleep
In a town without pity
Where the water runs deep
She said, "Be easy, baby
There ain't nothin' worth stealin' in here"

You're the one I've been looking for
You're the one that's got the key
But I can't figure out whether I'm too good for you
Or you're too good for me

有人见到我的爱人吗
有人见到我的爱人吗
有人见到我的爱人吗
我不知道
有人见到我的爱人吗？

你有话要跟我说
直说吧
无论你说什么
都不会给我打击
一定是我哪里做错了
你只要对我耳语就好
蝴蝶夫人[1]
她哄我睡觉
在一个没有怜悯的小镇
那里水流深深
她说："放松孩子
这儿没什么值得偷的"

你是我一直要找的人
你是那个有钥匙的人
但我搞不清楚是你配不上我
还是我配不上你

---

[1] 蝴蝶夫人，意大利作曲家普契尼的歌剧《蝴蝶夫人》中的女主角。

Has anybody seen my love
Has anybody seen my love
Has anybody seen my love
I don't know
Has anybody seen my love?

Well, they're not showing any lights tonight
And there's no moon
There's just a hot-blooded singer
Singing "Memphis in June"
While they're beatin' the devil out of a guy
Who's wearing a powder-blue wig
Later he'll be shot
For resisting arrest
I can still hear his voice crying
In the wilderness
What looks large from a distance
Close up ain't never that big

Never could learn to drink that blood
And call it wine
Never could learn to hold you, love
And call you mine

有人见到我的爱人吗
有人见到我的爱人吗
有人见到我的爱人吗
我不知道
有人见到我的爱人吗?

唉，今夜他们没亮出一点儿光
也没有月亮
只有一个热血歌手
在唱着《六月的孟菲斯》
这时他们正在把一个伙计揍得半死
他戴着淡蓝色的假发
稍后因为拒捕
他将被警察枪杀
我依然能听见他呼喊的声音
在旷野里
离远看很巨大的东西
凑近看却未必

永未能学会饮血
还把它叫作酒
永未能学会抱你，亲爱的
还说你是我的

## SEEING THE REAL YOU AT LAST

Well, I thought that the rain would cool things down
But it looks like it don't
I'd like to get you to change your mind
But it looks like you won't

From now on I'll be busy
Ain't goin' nowhere fast
I'm just glad it's over
And I'm seeing the real you at last

Well, didn't I risk my neck for you
Didn't I take chances?
Didn't I rise above it all for you
The most unfortunate circumstances?

Well, I have had some rotten nights
Didn't think that they would pass
I'm just thankful and grateful
To be seeing the real you at last

## 终于看见真的你

哦，我以为雨水会平息一切
可看来它没有
我想让你改变主意
可看来你不会

从现在起我要忙起来了
一时哪儿也去不了
我很高兴事情结束了
终于看见真的你

哦，我不是为你冒了生命危险吗
我不是接受了机会的挑战吗？
我不是摆脱了这最不济的逆境吗
全为了你？

哦，我经历过一些糜烂的夜
以为它们永远不会过去
现在我只觉得庆幸又感激
终于看见真的你

---

[1] 本首歌词多处源自电影台词，尤其黑色电影和西部片电影台词。

I'm hungry and I'm irritable
And I'm tired of this bag of tricks
At one time there was nothing wrong with me
That you could not fix

Well, I sailed through the storm
Strapped to the mast
But the time has come
And I'm seeing the real you at last

When I met you, baby
You didn't show no visible scars
You could ride like Annie Oakley
You could shoot like Belle Starr

Well, I don't mind a reasonable amount of trouble
Trouble always comes to pass
But all I care about now

我又饥饿又暴躁
对这些把戏感到厌烦
以前我身上的所有毛病
你都可以医治

哦，我曾把自己绑在桅杆上[1]
穿过了风暴
但那时刻到了
终于看见真的你

当我遇见你时，宝贝
你的身上没有可见的疤痕
你会像安妮·奥克利[2]那样骑马
像贝尔·斯塔尔[3]那样射击

哦，我不在乎一定的困难
困难总会过去
但我现在在乎的

---

[1] “把自己绑在桅杆上”见于多个历史或文学场景，最著名的是在《奥德赛》中，奥德修斯在航海时，为了在海妖塞壬诱人灭亡的歌声中生还，一度把自己绑在桅杆上。

[2] 安妮·奥克利（1860—1926），美国“水牛比尔”马戏团女明星，是个著名的神枪手、马术师，但不幸在一次火车意外中受伤，结束了演出生涯。音乐剧名作《安妮，拿起你的枪》即以她为原型。

[3] 贝尔·斯塔尔（1848—1889），具有传奇色彩的美国西部女匪，从事过马贼、走私等各种违法营生，有“强盗女王”之称。1941 年美国曾拍摄其传记片，中文名为《女罗宾汉》。

Is that I'm seeing the real you at last

Well, I'm gonna quit this baby talk now
I guess I should have known
I got troubles, I think maybe you got troubles
I think maybe we'd better leave each other alone

Whatever you gonna do
Please do it fast
I'm still trying to get used to
Seeing the real you at last

是终于看见真的你

哦，我将停止这孩子气的话
我想我该早一点懂得
我有麻烦，我想也许你也有麻烦
我想也许最好我们各自待着

不管你要做什么
请赶紧做
我依然在努力习惯
终于看见真的你

## I'LL REMEMBER YOU

I'll remember you
When I've forgotten all the rest
You to me were true
You to me were the best
When there is no more
You cut to the core
Quicker than anyone I knew
When I'm all alone
In the great unknown
I'll remember you

I'll remember you
At the end of the trail
I had so much left to do
I had so little time to fail
There's some people that
You don't forget
Even though you've only seen 'm one time or two
When the roses fade

# 我会记得你

我会记得你
当我忘记了别的一切
你对我是真实
你对我是第一
当一切都已不再
你切入了核心
比我认识的任何人都快
当我孤身一人
在巨大的未知中
我会记得你

我会记得你
在小路的尽头
那么多的事情要做
那么少的时间容许失败
有一些人
你没有忘记
即便你只见过他们一两次[1]
当玫瑰凋落

[1] “有一些人……你只见过他们一两次”，改编自鲍嘉主演的电影《夜长梦多》中一个角色对鲍嘉说的台词。

And I'm in the shade
I'll remember you

Didn't I, didn't I try to love you?
Didn't I, didn't I try to care?
Didn't I sleep, didn't I weep beside you
With the rain blowing in your hair?

I'll remember you
When the wind blows through the piney wood
It was you who came right through
It was you who understood
Though I'd never say
That I done it the way
That you'd have liked me to
In the end
My dear sweet friend
I'll remember you

而我在阴影中
我会记得你

我有没有，我有没有努力地爱你？
我有没有，我有没有努力地珍惜？
我有没有在你身旁睡去、哭泣
当那雨水，吹进你的发丝？

我会记得你
当风吹过松林
是你径直走来
是你懂得
虽然我绝不会说
我的所作所为
都如你期许
最后
我亲爱的甜蜜的朋友
我会记得你

# CLEAN-CUT KID

Everybody wants to know why he couldn't adjust
Adjust to what, a dream that bust?

He was a clean-cut kid
But they made a killer out of him
That's what they did

They said what's up is down, they said what isn't is
They put ideas in his head he thought were his

He was a clean-cut kid
But they made a killer out of him
That's what they did

He was on the baseball team, he was in the marching band
When he was ten years old he had a watermelon stand

He was a clean-cut kid

## 干干净净的孩子 [1]

每个人都纳闷为什么他无法适应
适应什么？一个破碎的梦？

他是个干干净净的孩子
他们却把他变成了一个杀手
这就是他们干的事

他们说上就是下，他们说不是就是是
他们把思想灌进他脑子，他以为是他想的

他是个干干净净的孩子
他们却把他变成了一个杀手
这就是他们干的事

他在棒球队，他在仪仗队
他在十岁的时候有了一个西瓜摊

他是个干干净净的孩子

---

[1] 歌词讲述了普通的美国年轻人在越战中经历的剧烈改变，评论家罗伯特·克里斯戈称之为“迄今最尖锐的越战老兵之歌”。本篇由郝佳校译。

But they made a killer out of him
That's what they did

He went to church on Sunday, he was a Boy Scout
For his friends he would turn his pockets inside out

He was a clean-cut kid
But they made a killer out of him
That's what they did

They said, "Listen boy, you're just a pup"
They sent him to a napalm health spa to shape up

They gave him dope to smoke, drinks and pills
A jeep to drive, blood to spill

They said "Congratulations, you got what it takes"
They sent him back into the rat race without any brakes

He was a clean-cut kid
But they made a killer out of him
That's what they did

He bought the American dream but it put him in debt
The only game he could play was Russian roulette

他们却把他变成了一个杀手
这就是他们干的事

他礼拜天去教堂，他是一名童子军
为朋友他会把口袋翻个里朝外

他是个干干净净的孩子
他们却把他变成了一个杀手
这就是他们干的事

他们说："听着小子，你还太嫩"
他们送他到汽油弹保健水疗地成长

他们给他大麻抽，给酒和药丸
给他吉普开，让鲜血四溅

他们说："祝贺你，你通过了"
他们把他送回玩命的竞赛，不带任何刹车

他是个干干净净的孩子
他们却把他变成了一个杀手
这就是他们干的事

他买了美国梦，可这让他负债累累
他唯一能玩的游戏，是俄罗斯轮盘赌

He drank Coca-Cola, he was eating Wonder Bread
Ate Burger Kings, he was well fed

He went to Hollywood to see Peter O'Toole
He stole a Rolls-Royce and drove it in a swimming pool

They took a clean-cut kid
And they made a killer out of him
That's what they did

He could've sold insurance, owned a restaurant or bar
Could've been an accountant or a tennis star

He was wearing boxing gloves, took a dive one day
Off the Golden Gate Bridge into China Bay

His mama walks the floor, his daddy weeps and moans
They gotta sleep together in a home they don't own

They took a clean-cut kid
And they made a killer out of him
That's what they did

他喝可口可乐，吃奇迹牌面包
食汉堡王，吃得可真不赖

他去好莱坞，看彼得·奥图尔[1]
他偷了辆劳斯莱斯，开进了游泳池

他们把一个干干净净的孩子
变成了一个杀手
这就是他们干的事

他本可卖保险，拥有一家餐厅或酒吧
本可成为会计或网球明星

他戴着拳套，有一天佯作被击倒
从金门大桥，扎进了中国湾[2]

他的妈妈踱来踱去，爸爸流泪呻吟
他们得一起睡在一个不属于自己的家

他们把一个干干净净的孩子
变成了一个杀手
这就是他们干的事

---

[1] 彼得·奥图尔，英国舞台剧演员，在电影《阿拉伯的劳伦斯》（1962）中把劳伦斯一角刻画得非常成功，驰名国际。

[2] 中国湾，代指渤海湾。

Well, everybody's asking why he couldn't adjust
All he ever wanted was somebody to trust

They took his head and turned it inside out
He never did know what it was all about

He had a steady job, he joined the choir
He never did plan to walk the high wire

They took a clean-cut kid
And they made a killer out of him
That's what they did

呃，每一个人都问他为什么无法适应
而他需要的只是，一个可以信任的人

他们把他的脑袋翻了个里朝外
他永远都不知道，这一切是怎么回事

他有了一份稳定的工作，他加入了唱诗班
他从未打算在高空中走索

他们把一个干干净净的孩子
变成了一个杀手
这就是他们干的事

## NEVER GONNA BE THE SAME AGAIN

Now you're here beside me, baby
You're a living dream
And every time you get this close
It makes me want to scream
You touched me and you knew
That I was warm for you and then
I ain't never gonna be the same again

Sorry if I hurt you, baby
Sorry if I did
Sorry if I touched the place
Where your secrets are hid
But you meant more than everything
And I could not pretend
I ain't never gonna be the same again

You give me something to think about, baby
Every time I see ya
Don't worry, baby, I don't mind leaving

# 永远不一样了[1]

现在你就在我身边，宝贝
是一个栩栩如生的梦
每次你离我这么近
都让我想要尖叫
你抚摸我并且知道
我为你而激动，然后
我会永远不一样了

抱歉若我伤了你，宝贝
抱歉若真是如此
抱歉若我触到了
你隐藏秘密之地
但你的意义超过一切
而我不能假装
我会永远不一样了

每一次见面，宝贝
你都令我有所思量
别担心宝贝，我不在意离去

---

[1] 本篇由郝佳校译。

I'd just like it to be my idea

You taught me how to love you, baby
You taught me, oh, so well
Now, I can't go back to what was, baby
I can't unring the bell
You took my reality
And cast it to the wind
And I ain't never gonna be the same again

我只是希望那是我自己的主意[1]

你教我如何爱你，宝贝
你教我，啊，教得多么好
如今，我无法恢复原状了，宝贝
我不能让钟声倒回去
你拿走了我的现实
把它掷向风
我会永远不一样了

[1] 我不在意离去/我只是希望那是我自己的主意，美国西部片《原野奇侠》（1953）中的台词。

## TRUST YOURSELF

Trust yourself
Trust yourself to do the things that only you know best
Trust yourself
Trust yourself to do what's right and not be second-guessed
Don't trust me to show you beauty
When beauty may only turn to rust
If you need somebody you can trust, trust yourself

Trust yourself
Trust yourself to know the way that will prove true in the end
Trust yourself
Trust yourself to find the path where there is no if and when
Don't trust me to show you the truth
When the truth may only be ashes and dust
If you want somebody you can trust, trust yourself

Well, you're on your own, you always were
In a land of wolves and thieves
Don't put your hope in ungodly man
Or be a slave to what somebody else believes

## 信你自己[1]

信你自己
信你自己去做只有你最了解的事
信你自己
信你自己会做正确的事，不被事后猜测
不要信我会给你展示美
既然美可能只会生锈
如果你需要信什么人，信你自己

信你自己
信你自己会知晓终可证明为真之道
信你自己
信你自己找得到那没有“如果”“既然”的途径
不要信我会给你呈现真理
既然真理可能只是尘与灰
如果你需要信什么人，信你自己

是啊，你独自面对，你一直如此
在群狼与众贼之地
别把希望寄托于不敬虔的人
也不要做他人之信的奴隶

[1] 本篇由郝佳校译。

Trust yourself
And you won't be disappointed when vain people let you down
Trust yourself
And look not for answers where no answers can be found
Don't trust me to show you love
When my love may be only lust
If you want somebody you can trust, trust yourself

信你自己
由此再不会为无谓的人让你失望而沮丧
信你自己
由此不再寻找答案在找不到答案的地方
不要信我会让你看到爱
既然我的爱可能只是欲望
如果你需要信什么人，信你自己

## EMOTIONALLY YOURS

Come baby, find me, come baby, remind me of where I once begun
Come baby, show me, show me you know me, tell me you're the one
I could be learning, you could be yearning to see behind closed doors
But I will always be emotionally yours

Come baby, rock me, come baby, lock me into the shadows of your heart
Come baby, teach me, come baby, reach me, let the music start
I could be dreaming but I keep believing you're the one I'm livin' for
And I will always be emotionally yours

It's like my whole life never happened
When I see you, it's as if I never had a thought
I know this dream, it might be crazy
But it's the only one I've got

Come baby, shake me, come baby, take me, I would be satisfied
Come baby, hold me, come baby, help me, my arms are open wide

## 充满感情的，你的[1]

来宝贝来找我，来宝贝提醒我，提醒我从哪儿开始
来宝贝向我表明，表明你了解我，证明你就是那一个
我也许在学习，你也许在向往，探究那闭门后的事
而我将永远是充满感情的，你的

来宝贝摇晃我，来宝贝锁上我，把我锁进你的心影
来宝贝来教我，来宝贝抓住我，让那音乐现在开始
我也许在做梦，但一直都相信，你是我为之而生的人
而我将永远是充满感情的，你的

就好像我的一生从没有发生
当我看见你，就好像我从没有过想法
我知道这个梦，它也许太疯狂
但这是我做过的唯一一个

来宝贝晃动我，来宝贝带上我，我将会感到多么满意
来宝贝抱紧我，来宝贝帮帮我，我的双臂张得那么辽阔

---

[1] 在英文书信最后署名时，写信人会按惯用格式写上“你的忠实的”“你的诚挚的”等等，本诗标题和诗中语句“emotionally yours”，即采用了这种格式。为与全诗诗韵、节奏相协调，拙译为“充满感情的，你的”。本篇由郝佳校译。

I could be unraveling wherever I'm traveling, even to foreign shores

But I will always be emotionally yours

我不会再迷乱了，不管走到哪里，哪怕到了异国海岸
而我将永远是充满感情的，你的

## WHEN THE NIGHT COMES FALLING FROM THE SKY

Look out across the fields, see me returning
Smoke is in your eye, you draw a smile
From the fireplace where my letters to you are burning
You've had time to think about it for a while

Well, I've walked two hundred miles, now look me over
It's the end of the chase and the moon is high
It won't matter who loves who
You'll love me or I'll love you
When the night comes falling from the sky

I can see through your walls and I know you're hurting
Sorrow covers you up like a cape
Only yesterday I know that you've been flirting
With disaster that you managed to escape

I can't provide for you no easy answers
Who are you that I should have to lie?
You'll know all about it, love
It'll fit you like a glove

## 当黑夜从天空落下[1]

眺望田野，看见我回来
烟雾在你眼中，你露出一丝微笑
壁炉里，我给你的信在燃烧
你有了些时间，想了一会儿

啊，我走了两百英里，瞧我
那追逐结束了，月亮高高悬起
谁爱谁都没关系
你会爱我，或者我会爱你
当黑夜从天空落下

我能看穿你的壁垒，知道你很受伤
悲哀正像斗篷，盖在你身上
直到昨天我才知道
你一直在与灾难周旋嬉戏，设法逃离

我无法为你提供简单的答案
你是什么人，我何必向你撒谎？
你会明白这一切的，爱人
它会贴合你像一只手套

---

[1] 本篇由郝佳、杨盈盈校译。

When the night comes falling from the sky

I can hear your trembling heart beat like a river
You must have been protecting someone last time I called
I've never asked you for nothing you couldn't deliver
I've never asked you to set yourself up for a fall

I saw thousands who could have overcome the darkness
For the love of a lousy buck, I've watched them die
Stick around, baby, we're not through
Don't look for me, I'll see you
When the night comes falling from the sky

In your teardrops, I can see my own reflection
It was on the northern border of Texas where I crossed the line
I don't want to be a fool starving for affection
I don't want to drown in someone else's wine

For all eternity I think I will remember
That icy wind that's howling in your eye
You will seek me and you'll find me
In the wasteland of your mind
When the night comes falling from the sky

Well, I sent you my feelings in a letter
But you were gambling for support

当黑夜从天空落下

我能听见你颤抖的心跳像一条河
上次我打电话，你必定是在护着谁
我从没要求过你不能付出的东西
我从没要求过你作茧自缚

我见过成千上万的人，本可战胜黑暗
却因为舍不下一两块臭钱，我看着他们死去
别离开我宝贝，我们还没完蛋
不要寻找我，我会看见你
当黑夜从天空落下

在你的泪珠中，我看见了自己的倒影
那是得克萨斯的北界，在那儿我穿过了边境
我不想做一个渴望爱情的傻瓜
我不想耽溺于别人的酒

永远永远，我想我会记住
那在你眼中咆哮的寒风
你将寻找我并且将寻见
我就在你心灵的荒原中
当黑夜从天空落下

哦，我将感情用信寄给你
可你在赌的是支持

This time tomorrow I'll know you better
When my memory is not so short

This time I'm asking for freedom
Freedom from a world which you deny
And you'll give it to me now
I'll take it anyhow
When the night comes falling from the sky

明天此时我将进一步认清你
到时我的记性不会太差

这回我会索要自由
从你否定的世界索要自由
而你一定要给我
不管怎样我一定会得到
当黑夜从天空落下

## SOMETHING'S BURNING, BABY

Something is burning, baby, are you aware?
Something is the matter, baby, there's smoke in your hair
Are you still my friend, baby, show me a sign
Is the love in your heart for me turning blind?

You've been avoiding the main streets for a long, long while
The truth that I'm seeking is in your missing file
What's your position, baby, what's going on?
Why is the light in your eyes nearly gone?

I know everything about this place, or so it seems
Am I no longer a part of your plans or your dreams?
Well, it is so obvious that something has changed
What's happening, baby, to make you act so strange?

Something is burning, baby, here's what I say
Even the bloodhounds of London couldn't find you today

## 什么东西着了，宝贝[1]

什么东西着了宝贝，你感觉到没有？
出事儿了宝贝，你的头发在冒烟
你还是我朋友吗宝贝，给我个表示
你心里对我的爱是否正变得茫然？

你避开那些大街已经很久很久
我要找的真相在你的遗失档案里
你是什么看法宝贝，发生了什么？
你眼中的光何以几近消失？

我熟知这个地方的一切，或者看来如此
我不再是你计划或梦想的一部分了？
好吧，很显然事情已经起了变化
发生了什么宝贝，你的举止变得如此陌生？

什么东西着了宝贝，这就是我要说的
即便是伦敦的寻血猎犬[2]今天也找不到你

---

[1] 本篇由郝佳校译。

[2] 寻血猎犬，一种以辨别人类气味著称的猎犬，以19世纪英国用其缉私为肇端，形象深入民心。开膛手一案中，苏格兰场即用其寻获凶手。

I see the shadow of a man, baby, makin' you blue
Who is he, baby, and what's he to you?

We've reached the edge of the road, baby, where the pasture begins
Where charity is supposed to cover up a multitude of sins
But where do you live, baby, and where is the light?
Why are your eyes just staring off in the night?

I can feel it in the night when I think of you
I can feel it in the light and it's got to be true
You can't live by bread alone, you won't be satisfied
You can't roll away the stone if your hands are tied

Got to start someplace, baby, can you explain?
Please don't fade away on me, baby, like the midnight train
Answer me, baby, a casual look will do
Just what in the world has come over you?

I can feel it in the wind and it's upside down
I can feel it in the dust as I get off the bus on the outskirts of town
I've had the Mexico City blues since the last hairpin curve

我看见一个人的影子宝贝，那让你变得忧郁
他是谁宝贝，他对你意味着什么？

我们已经到了路边宝贝，那边就是草场
那边爱应该能遮掩许多的罪
但是你住哪儿宝贝，灯在哪儿？
为什么你的眼在黑夜中直瞪着

我能在黑夜中感觉到，当我想起你
我能在光芒中感觉到，这一定是真的
你不能单靠面包活着，这你不会满意
你不能让石头滚开如果你的手被绑着

总要起个头宝贝，你能不能解释一下？
请不要从我身边消失宝贝，仿佛那午夜列车
回答我啊宝贝，随便一个眼神都可以
究竟是什么攫住了你？

我能在风中感觉到，它在翻覆
我能在尘土中感觉到，当我在城郊走下客车[1]
从上一个急转弯我就有了这墨西哥城蓝调[2]

---

[1] 美国歌手路易斯·乔丹有蓝调歌曲《我要搬到城郊》《我要在城郊离开你》，与下句的“蓝调”呼应。

[2] 杰克·凯鲁亚克著有诗集《墨西哥城蓝调》（1959）。据艾伦·金斯堡说，迪伦认为这是第一本用美式语言对他说话的书。

I don't wanna see you bleed, I know what you need but it ain't
what you deserve

Something is burning, baby, something's in flames
There's a man going 'round calling names
Ring down when you're ready, baby, I'm waiting for you
I believe in the impossible, you know that I do

我不想看你流血，我知道你要什么但这并非
　你应得

什么东西着了宝贝，有什么东西在火里
有一个人正在到处骂大街
你准备好了就打电话下来宝贝，我在等你
我相信不可能的事，你知道我真的信

## DARK EYES

Oh, the gentlemen are talking and the midnight moon is on the riverside
They're drinking up and walking and it is time for me to slide
I live in another world where life and death are memorized
Where the earth is strung with lovers' pearls and all I see are dark eyes

A cock is crowing far away and another soldier's deep in prayer
Some mother's child has gone astray, she can't find him anywhere
But I can hear another drum beating for the dead that rise
Whom nature's beast fears as they come and all I see are dark eyes

They tell me to be discreet for all intended purposes
They tell me revenge is sweet and from where they stand, I'm sure it is
But I feel nothing for their game where beauty goes unrecognized
All I feel is heat and flame and all I see are dark eyes

Oh, the French girl, she's in paradise and a drunken man is at the wheel
Hunger pays a heavy price to the falling gods of speed and steel

## 黑暗的眼睛[1]

哦，绅士们在交谈，午夜的月亮挂在河边
他们边干杯边闲走这正是我溜走的时机
我住在另一个世界那里生与死都被铭记
那里地球和情人的珍珠串在一起我看见的全是黑暗的眼睛

远处传来了鸡鸣，又一个士兵在深深祷告
有个孩子走入迷途，他的母亲到处都寻他不到
但我能听见又一面鼓为了让死者复活在敲
当他们走来野兽惊惧我看见的全是黑暗的眼睛

他们告诫我对一切预定目标都要深思熟虑
他们告诫我复仇是甜蜜的，从他们的角度看当然如此
但我对他们的游戏毫无感觉，那里美变得不可辨认
我感到的只是热和火我看见的全是黑暗的眼睛

哦，法兰西女郎上了天堂，一个醉汉掌着方向盘
为速度与钢铁的坠落之神饥饿付出了沉重代价

---

[1] 据早期访谈和迪伦的《编年史》（第一卷），制作人阿瑟·贝克建议专辑《帝国滑稽剧》以较简单的歌曲作结，于是迪伦创作了这首歌。迪伦半夜步出位于曼哈顿的酒店电梯时，看到一个应召女郎在过道上走来："……她有着蓝色眼影，黑眼线，黑暗的眼睛。"这成了迪伦创作这首歌词的灵感。

Oh, time is short and the days are sweet and passion rules the arrow that flies
A million faces at my feet but all I see are dark eyes

哦，时光短促日子甜蜜激情统治着飞矢

一百万张脸在我脚下，我看见的全是黑暗的眼睛

KNOCKED
LOAD

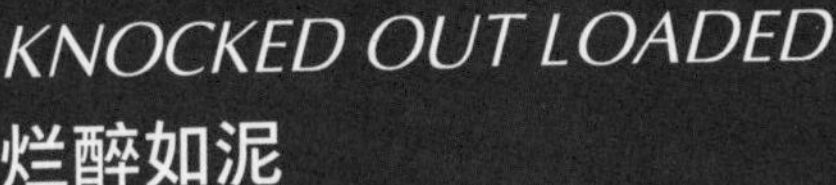

# KNOCKED OUT LOADED
# 烂醉如泥

漂离岸边太远

也许有天

布朗斯维尔姑娘

中了你的魔咒

附加歌词

五指成拳，五人成团（时辰到了，兄弟！）

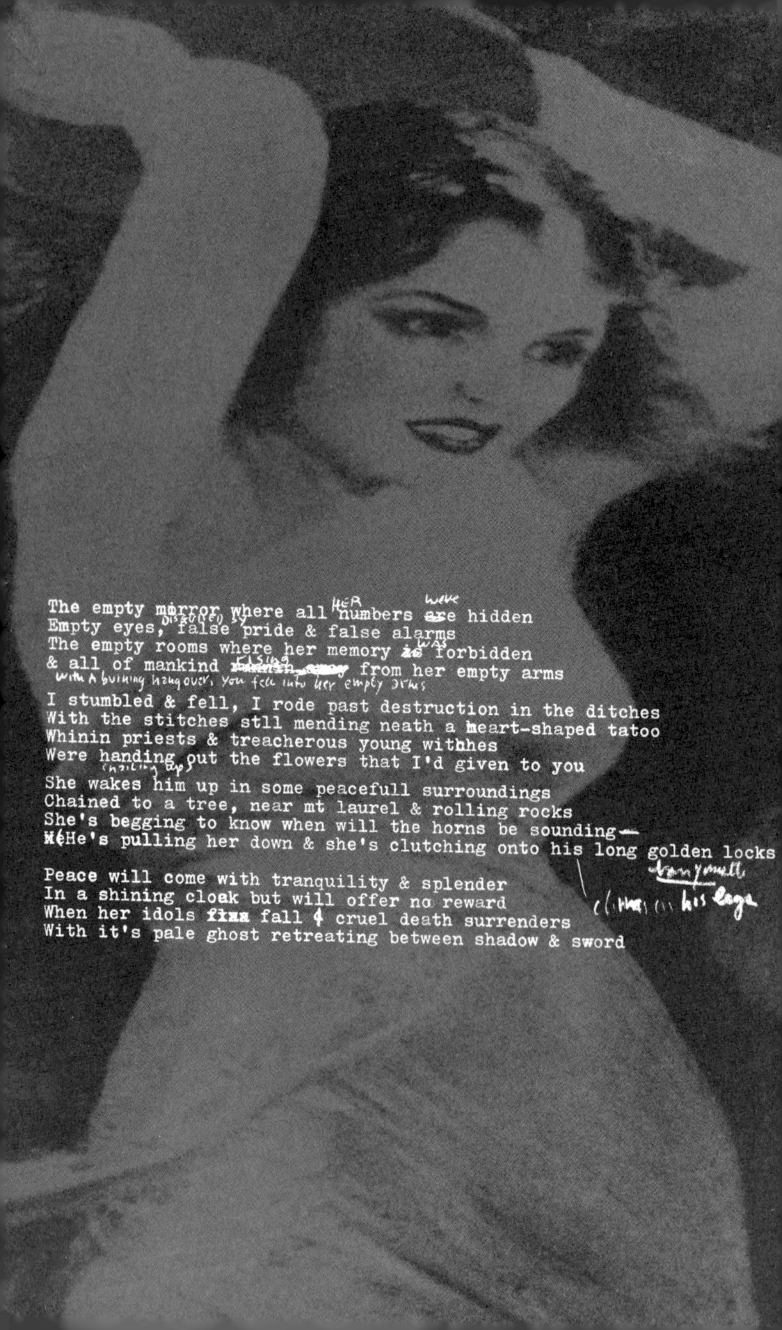
The empty mirror where all numbers hidden
Empty eyes, false pride & false alarms
The empty rooms where her memory forbidden
& all of mankind from her empty arms
I stumbled & fell, I rode past destruction in the ditches
With the stitches stll mending neath a heart-shaped tatoo
Whinin priests & treacherous young withhes
Were handing out the flowers that I'd given to you
She wakes him up in some peacefull surroundings
Chained to a tree, near mt laurel & rolling rocks
She's begging to know when will the horns be sounding
He's pulling her down & she's clutching onto his long golden locks
Peace will come with tranquility & splender
In a shining cloak but will offer no reward
When her idols fall & cruel death surrenders
With it's pale ghost retreating between shadow & sword

《烂醉如泥》是迪伦第24张录音室专辑，哥伦比亚唱片公司于1986年7月14日发行。

这张专辑既不叫好也不叫座，销量惨淡，评论大多负面。共含8首歌曲，全长35分14秒，仅此一项，即给人分量不足的印象。其中，迪伦独立署名的歌曲只有2首，另有3首与他人合作署名的歌曲、1首迪伦改编的民歌以及2首翻唱歌曲。[1] 专辑的制作时间长达2年。

1984年7月26日，《烂醉如泥》中的第1首歌——《漂离岸边太远》在纽约三角洲录音室定下了节奏音轨。12月，另一首原创曲目《布朗斯维尔姑娘》，此时还叫《新丹维尔姑娘》，在好莱坞彻罗基录音室现出雏形。又11个月过去，1985年11月20至23日，在伦敦教堂录音室，迪伦与卡罗尔·拜尔·塞杰尔合作了《中了你的魔咒》。

1986年春天，"真实告白"巡演在日本的最后一场音乐会结束，美国巡演的第一场尚未启动，4月28日至5月13日、5月19日、6月19日，在洛杉矶附近的2个不同录音室，迪伦又进行了大约22场录音。

---

[1] 本书仅收录其中4首歌曲及1首附加歌词。——编者注

历时2年，近30场录音，7位歌手、30余位音乐人、一个15人的少年合唱团，所有声音都是数码录制；参与阵容中有韵律操乐队（Eurythmics）灵魂人物斯图尔特，民谣头部明星“丁骨”伯内特、汤姆·佩蒂（Tom Petty）、克里斯·克里斯托弗森，滚石乐队吉他手罗尼·伍德（Ronnie Wood），参与多首迪伦经典的阿尔·库珀（Al Kooper）……这是跨越多个时空，最后通过数码技术便捷组装到一起的作品。

其间还发生了一件事：1986年6月4日，专辑发行前一个月，迪伦迎娶了第二任妻子、他的伴唱歌手卡罗琳·丹尼斯（Carolyn Dennis）。此前的1月31日，卡罗琳诞下二人的爱情结晶——女儿卡罗尔（Carol）。

1986年1月，一位记者曾采访迪伦，当时他刚与斯图尔特在后者的伦敦录音室、吸引众多新锐人物的音乐前沿，制作完成《中了你的魔咒》。迪伦对录制结果异常满意，觉得这张专辑会比《帝国滑稽剧》更棒，“录制的过程变得更加容易、迅速了，所以肯定会比上一张听上去更连贯。”

然而迪伦的乐观，以及各路风格迥异的名人加持，对《烂醉如泥》的面世结果都没有多大帮助。有人称它为“大杂烩”。迪伦后来对记者说的一句话，透露了他此时完全不同于以前的考量：“如果我的唱片无论如何都只能卖出某个定数，那么我何必要在制作上花那么多时间呢？”安东尼·德柯蒂斯（Anthony DeCurtis）撰文批评道：“它草率、拼凑的性质表明，迪伦发行这张唱片不是有什么特别的话要说，只是要在他1986年巡演期间赚点钱。”

但是近年来，这张专辑却在迪伦的歌迷中赢得了一批狂热追随者，它被认为是迪伦最不为人理解的作品，需要被重新认识。但批评界的共识一如既往，一些回顾仍视其为“迪伦专辑的绝对底部”“职业败笔”。

不过，确实有些方面值得思量。从背景上，它发生在数码录音——新浪潮的时代，迪伦受到录音工业新变化、新风尚的冲击，可能产生了不同以往的思考。它确实是张“杂烩”，汇集了多方合作，而不是概念唱片，不求一人一辑的纯正。这在迪伦的创作生涯中从未有过，此后也再未出现。从专辑封面看，迪伦的思路也相当怪异，竟由一张 20 世纪 30 年代的低俗杂志封面《下流冒险故事》改造而成：一位肉感少女，举着陶罐砸向正扼住一个男人喉咙的土匪。画面极其恶俗，此等封面构思，也跳脱了迪伦的思路。

迪伦与佩蒂合作的《我心已定》（“Got My Mind Made Up”）没有收在本诗集中。其他的 4 首创作中有 3 首是深陷爱情纠结的作品。其中，《也许有天》是首重量级情歌：有情到深处的苛责，也有仿佛跨越了一生的情谊。

至于《布朗斯维尔姑娘》，一直被视为不重要专辑中的重要之作。罗伯特·克里斯戈称其为“（迪伦）伟大的荒谬史诗中最伟大、最荒谬的”。诗中故事，可能指涉格利高里·派克主演的西部片《枪手》（*The Gunfighter*，1950）或《阳光下的决斗》（*Duel in the Sun*，1946），这首诗将叙述者经历与电影主角经历混合，使现实与虚构相互交错，具有现代小说的特征，且感人至深。

## DRIFTIN' TOO FAR FROM SHORE

I didn't know that you'd be leavin'
Or who you thought you were talkin' to
I figure maybe we're even
Or maybe I'm one up on you

I send you all my money
Just like I did before
I tried to reach you honey
But you're driftin' too far from shore

Driftin' too far from shore
Driftin' too far from shore
Driftin' too far from shore
Driftin' too far from shore

I ain't gonna get lost in this current
I don't like playing cat and mouse
No gentleman likes making love to a servant
Especially when he's in his father's house

I never could guess your weight, baby
Never needed to call you my whore

## 漂离岸边太远

当时我不知道你要走了
或者你以为你是在跟谁谈
我料想兴许我们扯平了
又兴许你对我有亏欠

寄给你我所有的钱
就像我以前所做的那样
努力地想够到你亲爱的
可是你漂离岸边太远

漂离岸边太远
漂离岸边太远
漂离岸边太远
漂离岸边太远

我不会在这激流中迷失
我不喜欢玩猫捉老鼠
没有哪位绅士会上一个女仆
特别是在他父亲屋里

你的体重我永远猜不对，宝贝
你是我的骚货我用不着这么喊

I always thought you were straight, baby
But you're driftin' too far from shore

Driftin' too far from shore
Driftin' too far from shore
Driftin' too far from shore
Driftin' too far from shore

Well these times and these tunnels are haunted
The bottom of the barrel is too
I waited years sometimes for what I wanted
Everybody can't be as lucky as you

Never no more do I wonder
Why you don't never play with me anymore
At any moment you could go under
'Cause you're driftin' too far from shore

Driftin' too far from shore
Driftin' too far from shore
Driftin' too far from shore
Driftin' too far from shore

You and me we had completeness
I give you all of what I could provide
We weren't on the wrong side, sweetness

我总以为你这人是直的，宝贝
可是你漂离岸边太远

漂离岸边太远
漂离岸边太远
漂离岸边太远
漂离岸边太远

哦这些地道这些时候总闹鬼
水桶底下也不消停
为偿所愿有时我一等数年
不可能每个人都有你这般幸运

我已经不再瞎琢磨了
为什么你不再跟我痴缠
你随时可能会沉下去
因为你漂离岸边太远

漂离岸边太远
漂离岸边太远
漂离岸边太远
漂离岸边太远

你我曾经有过圆满
我给了你我能付出的全部
我们不是犯了错误，心肝

We were the wrong side

I've already ripped out the phones, honey
You can't walk the streets in a war
I can finish this alone honey
You're driftin' too far from shore

我们就是那错误

我已经扯掉电话线，亲爱的
你不能在战争中逛大街
我会一个人结束这些亲爱的
你漂离岸边太远

# MAYBE SOMEDAY

Maybe someday you'll be satisfied
When you've lost everything you'll have nothing left to hide
When you're through running over things like you're walking 'cross
the tracks
Maybe you'll beg me to take you back
Maybe someday you'll find out everybody's somebody's fool
Maybe then you'll realize what it would have taken to keep me cool
Maybe someday when you're by yourself alone
You'll know the love that I had for you was never my own

Maybe someday you'll have nowhere to turn
You'll look back and wonder 'bout the bridges you have burned
You'll look back sometime when the lights grow dim
And you'll see you look much better with me than you do with him
Through hostile cities and unfriendly towns
Thirty pieces of silver, no money down
Maybe someday, you will understand
That something for nothing is everybody's plan

Maybe someday you'll remember what you felt

## 也许有天

也许有天你会知足
你失去了一切，再没什么要藏着掖着
你穿过世事就像穿过
　铁路
也许你会求我带你回去
也许有天你会发现每个人都是别人眼中的傻瓜
也许那时你就会懂得为了冷静我都付出什么
也许有天当你孑然一身
你就明白我对你的爱从不是我一个人的

也许有天你会无路可逃
你会回首往事，惊讶于你亲手烧掉的桥
灯光转暗时你会回忆
然后就发现你跟我远好过你跟他在一起
穿过敌意的城市和不友好的镇子
三十银币血钱[1]，零首付贷款
也许有天，你会恍然大悟
不劳而获是每人都在打的算盘

也许有天你会记起你的感觉

---

[1] 《圣经》中，犹大出卖耶稣，得血钱银币 30 块。

When there was blood on the moon in the cotton belt
When both of us, baby, were going through some sort of a test
Neither one of us could do what we do best
I should have known better, baby, I should have called your bluff
I guess I was too off the handle, not sentimental enough
Maybe someday, you'll believe me when I say
That I wanted you, baby, in every kind of way

Maybe someday you'll hear a voice from on high
Sayin', "For whose sake did you live, for whose sake did you die?"
Forgive me, baby, for what I didn't do
For not breakin' down no bedroom door to get at you
Always was a sucker for the right cross
Never wanted to go home 'til the last cent was lost
Maybe someday you will look back and see
That I made it so easy for you to follow me

Maybe someday there'll be nothing to tell
I'm just as happy as you, baby, I just can't say it so well
Never slumbered or slept or waited for lightning to strike
There's no excuse for you to say that we don't think alike
You said you were goin' to Frisco, stay a couple of months

当时在棉花带[1]，月亮泛着血
当时我们俩，宝贝，正经历某个考验
谁都不能一人做两人做得好的事
我本该更清楚，宝贝，我本该让你挑明
我想我也是失态，不够敏感多情
也许有天，你会相信我当我说
我要你，宝贝，以任何方式

也许有天你会听到高处有个声音
说："你生看谁的分儿上，你死又为了谁？"
原谅我吧，宝贝，为我没做到的事
为我没有破门而入去得到你[2]
为我一直是迷恋右勾拳的傻瓜
总是花光最后一分钱才想起回家
也许有天你回过头就会明白
我让你跟着我这实在是太轻易

也许有天会无话可说
我就和你一样幸福，宝贝，我只是说不清楚
从未打盹和睡去也从未等过雷劈
你没理由说我们想不到一起去
那次你说你要去旧金山待几个月

---

[1] 棉花带，美国东南部产棉区。

[2] 为我没有破门而入去得到你，美国电影《鸳鸯谱》（*Separate Tables*, 1958）中的台词。

I always like San Francisco, I was there for a party once

Maybe someday you'll see that it's true

There was no greater love than what I had for you

我一直喜欢圣弗朗西斯科[1]，以前聚会我去过

也许有天你会明白这是千真万确

比起我对你的爱再没什么爱是更伟大的

[1] 圣弗朗西斯科，即旧金山。前一句“你”说到旧金山，旧金山一词用简略口语。后一句“我”说的话，旧金山一词用了全称。“我”说的话，出自美国电影《旋涡之外》(*Out of the Past*，1947）的台词。

## BROWNSVILLE GIRL
(WITH SAM SHEPARD)

Well, there was this movie I seen one time
About a man riding 'cross the desert and it starred Gregory Peck
He was shot down by a hungry kid trying to make a name for himself
The townspeople wanted to crush that kid down and string him up by the neck

Well, the marshal, now he beat that kid to a bloody pulp
As the dying gunfighter lay in the sun and gasped for his last breath
"Turn him loose, let him go, let him say he outdrew me fair and square
I want him to feel what it's like to every moment face his death"

Well, I keep seeing this stuff and it just comes a-rolling in
And you know it blows right through me like a ball and chain
You know I can't believe we've lived so long and are still so far

## 布朗斯维尔[1]姑娘

（与萨姆·谢泼德合作）

哦，这部电影我看过一遍[2]
讲一个人骑马穿过沙漠，是格利高里·派克
　演的
他被一个想出名的饥饿少年开枪
　撂倒
镇上的人想把那孩子撕了，把绳子套在
　他脖子上

哦，警察局长，这会儿把那孩子打得血肉模糊
这枪手就要死了，瘫在阳光下喘最后
　一口气
“给他松绑，放他走，让他公平公正说拔枪
　比我快
我要叫他感受时时刻刻面对死亡的感觉”

哦，我看着这玩意儿，它就这样滚滚而来
你知道它就像是一条锁链将我击穿
你知道我无法相信我们活了这么久相距却仍

---

[1] 布朗斯维尔，美国得克萨斯州南部城市，位于美墨边境。

[2] 所指电影为美国西部片《枪手》（1950）。

apart
The memory of you keeps callin' after me like a rollin' train

I can still see the day that you came to me on the painted desert
In your busted down Ford and your platform heels
I could never figure out why you chose that particular place to meet
Ah, but you were right. It was perfect as I got in behind the wheel

Well, we drove that car all night into San Anton'
And we slept near the Alamo, your skin was so tender and soft
Way down in Mexico you went out to find a doctor and you never came back
I would have gone on after you but I didn't feel like letting my head get blown off

Well, we're drivin' this car and the sun is comin' up over the Rockies
Now I know she ain't you but she's here and she's got that dark rhythm in her soul
But I'm too over the edge and I ain't in the mood anymore to remember the times when I was your only man
And she don't want to remind me. She knows this car would go

这么远
对你的记忆就像滚滚的火车在我身后不停呼唤

我仍然记得那天你在彩色沙漠[1]找到我
开着破福特穿着厚底儿靴
我永远搞不懂你为什么选那个地方
见面
啊，但你是对的。完美啊当我坐到
方向盘前

哦，我们一整夜开着车到了圣安东
睡在阿拉莫附近，你的肌肤如此柔软
一路去墨西哥，你出去找医生然后
就再没回来
我本可以去追你但我不想我的脑袋
被人打烂

哦，我们开着这车，太阳在落基山
升起
这会儿我知道她不是你但她就在这儿，
她灵魂中有那种黑暗韵律
可我太过分了，再没心情回忆我是你
唯一男人的时光
她也不想提醒我。她知道这车会失去

[1] 彩色沙漠，位于美国亚利桑那州东北部。

out of control

Brownsville girl with your Brownsville curls
Teeth like pearls shining like the moon above
Brownsville girl, show me all around the world
Brownsville girl, you're my honey love

Well, we crossed the panhandle and then we headed towards Amarillo
We pulled up where Henry Porter used to live. He owned a wreckin' lot outside of town about a mile
Ruby was in the backyard hanging clothes, she had her red hair tied back. She saw us come rolling up in a trail of dust
She said, "Henry ain't here but you can come on in, he'll be back in a little while"

Then she told us how times were tough and about how she was thinkin' of bummin' a ride back to from where she started
But ya know, she changed the subject every time money came up
She said, "Welcome to the land of the living dead."
You could tell she was so broken hearted
She said, "Even the swap meets around here are getting pretty corrupt"

控制

布朗斯维尔姑娘有着你布朗斯维尔的卷发
皓齿如珍珠闪亮如高高在上的明月
布朗斯维尔姑娘，带我走过全世界
布朗斯维尔姑娘，你是我亲密的爱人

哦，我们穿过了锅把区[1]，然后奔往
阿马里洛
在亨利·波特住过的地方停下。城外大约一英里
有他的破房子
露比在后院晾衣服，红头发扎在脑后。
她见我们卷起一路尘土而来
她说："亨利不在不过你们进来吧，
他一会儿就回来"

然后她告诉我们时世艰难，说她想搭车
回她出来的地方
但是你知道，每次一提钱她就转移
话题
她说："欢迎来到活死人之地。"
你看得出她心都碎了
她说："就连这里的旧货市场也变得
要烂掉了"

[1] 锅把区，美国得克萨斯州北部的柄状狭长区域。

"How far are y'all going?" Ruby asked us with a sigh
"We're going all the way 'til the wheels fall off and burn
'Til the sun peels the paint and the seat covers fade and the water moccasin dies"
Ruby just smiled and said, "Ah, you know some babies never learn"

Something about that movie though, well I just can't get it out of my head
But I can't remember why I was in it or what part I was supposed to play
All I remember about it was Gregory Peck and the way people moved
And a lot of them seemed to be lookin' my way

Brownsville girl with your Brownsville curls
Teeth like pearls shining like the moon above
Brownsville girl, show me all around the world
Brownsville girl, you're my honey love

Well, they were looking for somebody with a pompadour
I was crossin' the street when shots rang out
I didn't know whether to duck or to run, so I ran

“你们要走多远？”露比叹息着问
“我们会一路走，直到轮子掉下来燃烧
直到太阳剥落车漆，座套褪色，水蝮蛇
　死掉”
露比只笑着说：“啊你看，有些后生就是
　不学好”

不过是那电影中的一些事，哦我就是无法
　从脑中驱除
但我不记得我为什么会在里面，我演的又是
　哪个角色
只记得格利高里·派克以及人们的
　举手投足
他们中很多人似乎都在看着我

布朗斯维尔姑娘有着你布朗斯维尔的卷发
皓齿如珍珠闪亮如高高在上的明月
布朗斯维尔姑娘，带我走过全世界
布朗斯维尔姑娘，你是我亲密的爱人

哦，他们在找一个留蓬帕杜发型[1]的人
枪声响起时我正穿过街道
我不知该躲还是该跑，所以我跑了

---

[1] 蓬帕杜发型，即“猫王”的发型。

"We got him cornered in the churchyard," I heard somebody
shout

Well, you saw my picture in the *Corpus Christi Tribune.*
Underneath it, it said, "A man with no alibi"
You went out on a limb to testify for me, you said I was with
you
Then when I saw you break down in front of the judge and cry
real tears
It was the best acting I saw anybody do

Now I've always been the kind of person that doesn't like to
trespass but sometimes you just find yourself over the line
Oh if there's an original thought out there, I could use it right
now
You know, I feel pretty good, but that ain't sayin' much.
I could feel a whole lot better
If you were just here by my side to show me how

Well, I'm standin' in line in the rain to see a movie starring
Gregory Peck
Yeah, but you know it's not the one that I had in mind
He's got a new one out now, I don't even know what it's about
But I'll see him in anything so I'll stand in line

Brownsville girl with your Brownsville curls

“我们把他逼教堂墓地里了。” 我听见有人
  喊道

哦，你在《科珀斯克里斯蒂论坛报》看了我的照片。
  照片下说明 :“一个无不在场证明者”
你冒险为我做证，说我和你
  在一起
然后我看到你在法官面前崩溃并流下
  真的眼泪
这是我见过的最好的表演

喏我一直是那种不爱乱来的，
  但有时你会发现你越界了
啊如果哪儿有个原创想法，我立即就会
  采用它
你知道，我觉得很好，但这并不说明什么。
如果你就在我身边告诉我如何做
我会整个感觉好很多

哦，我在雨中排队看格利高里 · 派克
  主演的电影
是啊，但你知道这不是我心里的那部
他现在出了个新的，我都不知道它讲什么
可我就是想看他，所以我排队，随便什么

布朗斯维尔姑娘有着你布朗斯维尔的卷发

Teeth like pearls shining like the moon above
Brownsville girl, show me all around the world
Brownsville girl, you're my honey love

You know, it's funny how things never turn out the way you had 'em planned
The only thing we knew for sure about Henry Porter is that his name wasn't Henry Porter
And you know there was somethin' about you baby that I liked that was always too good for this world
Just like you always said there was somethin' about me you liked that I left behind in the French Quarter

Strange how people who suffer together have stronger connections than people who are most content
I don't have any regrets, they can talk about me plenty when I'm gone
You always said people don't do what they believe in, they just do what's most convenient, then they repent
And I always said, "Hang on to me, baby, and let's hope that the roof stays on"

There was a movie I seen one time, I think I sat through it twice
I don't remember who I was or where I was bound
All I remember about it was it starred Gregory Peck, he wore a gun and he was shot in the back

皓齿如珍珠闪亮如高高在上的明月
布朗斯维尔姑娘，带我走过全世界
布朗斯维尔姑娘，你是我亲密的爱人

你知道，万事不会如你计划的发展，
　这很好玩
这个亨利·波特，我们唯一确定的是他的
　姓名不是亨利·波特
你知道你身上有些我喜欢的东西宝贝，
　对这世界来说这总是太好
就像你总说我身上有些你喜欢的，
　被我留在了法国区

奇怪的是一起苦的人会比最满足的人有
　更牢靠的关系
我毫无遗憾，我走后他们可对我
　大谈特谈
你总是说人们不做他们相信的事，
　只行他们最方便的事，然后就后悔
而我总是说："跟牢我宝贝，
　但愿屋顶还在上面"

有一部电影我看过一遍，我想我看了两遍
我忘了我是谁，我曾在哪里
只记得它是格利高里·派克主演的，他带着枪，
　背后中弹

Seems like a long time ago, long before the stars were torn
down

Brownsville girl with your Brownsville curls
Teeth like pearls shining like the moon above
Brownsville girl, show me all around the world
Brownsville girl, you're my honey love

仿佛是很久以前，早在星星被扯下
　之前

布朗斯维尔姑娘有着你布朗斯维尔的卷发
皓齿如珍珠闪亮如高高在上的明月
布朗斯维尔姑娘，带我走过全世界
布朗斯维尔姑娘，你是我亲密的爱人

# UNDER YOUR SPELL
(WITH CAROL BAYER SAGER)

Somethin' about you that I can't shake
Don't know how much more of this I can take
Baby, I'm under your spell

I was knocked out and loaded in the naked night
When my last dream exploded, I noticed your light
Baby, oh what a story I could tell

It's been nice seeing you, you read me like a book
If you ever want to reach me, you know where to look
Baby, I'll be at the same hotel

I'd like to help you but I'm in a bit of a jam
I'll call you tomorrow if there's phones where I am
Baby, caught between heaven and hell

But I will be back, I will survive
You'll never get rid of me as long as you're alive
Baby, can't you tell

Well it's four in the morning by the sound of the birds

## 中了你的魔咒

（与卡罗尔·拜尔·塞杰尔合作）

你的有些事儿我忘不掉
真不知道我还能承受多少
宝贝儿，我中了你的魔咒

赤裸裸的夜我烂醉如泥
当最后的梦爆掉，我注意到了你的灯
宝贝儿，啊我会说，这是个多棒的故事

见到你真好，你读我就像读书
若你要联系我，你知道去哪儿找
宝贝儿，我还住在那家旅店

我很想帮你可我遇上点儿麻烦
我住的地方若有电话明天我打给你
宝贝儿，我困在天堂地狱之间

但我会回来，我能活下去
只要你活着，你就休想摆脱我
宝贝儿，你看不出来吗

哦已是凌晨四点外面响起了鸟鸣

I'm starin' at your picture, I'm hearin' your words
Baby, they ring in my head like a bell

Everywhere you go it's enough to break hearts
Someone always gets hurt, a fire always starts
You were too hot to handle, you were breaking every vow
I trusted you baby, you can trust me now

Turn back baby, wipe your eye
Don't think I'm leaving here without a kiss goodbye
Baby, is there anything left to tell?

I'll see you later when I'm not so out of my head
Maybe next time I'll let the dead bury the dead
Baby, what more can I tell?

Well the desert is hot, the mountain is cursed
Pray that I don't die of thirst
Baby, two feet from the well

我盯着你的相片，听着你的说话声
宝贝儿，它像铃儿一般在我脑中回旋

无论你去哪儿都足以让人心碎
总有人会受伤，一团火总是燃起
你真烫手啊握不住，句句誓言你都打破
以前我信你宝贝儿，现在你可以信我

回过身来宝贝儿，擦去泪水
没有吻别别想我会离去
宝贝儿，你还有什么话没说？

等我不那么崩溃时我就去找你
也许下一次我就会让死人埋死人
宝贝儿，我还能说什么呢？

哦沙漠炽热，山被诅咒
但愿我不会渴死
宝贝儿，离水井只差两英尺

## BAND OF THE HAND
## (IT'S HELL TIME, MAN!)

Band of the hand
Band of the hand
Band of the hand
Band of the hand

Down these streets the fools rule
There's no freedom or self respect
A knife's point or a trip to the joint
Is about all you can expect

They kill people here who stand up for their rights
The system's just too damned corrupt
It's always the same, the name of the game
Is who do you know higher up

Band of the hand
Band of the hand
Band of the hand

## 五指成拳，五人成团
## （时辰到了，兄弟！）[1]

五指成拳，五人成团
五指成拳，五人成团
五指成拳，五人成团
五指成拳，五人成团

在这些蠢货把控的街道
无所谓自由和个人尊严
玩玩儿刀或去去夜店
几乎就是你所有的期盼

他们杀掉了捍卫自己权利的人
体制实在太他娘的腐败
总是那同一出，游戏的名字
是“谁认识的人更厉害”

五指成拳，五人成团
五指成拳，五人成团
五指成拳，五人成团

---

[1] 这首歌是迪伦为美国同名电影（中文译名《四海小兄弟》）而作，所述内容与影片情节有关。

Band of the hand

The blacks and the whites
Steal the other kids' lives
Wealth is a filthy rag
So erotic so unpatriotic
So wrapped up in the American flag

The witchcraft scum exploiting the dumb
Turns children into crooks and slaves
Whose heroes and healers are real stoned dealers
Who should be put in their graves

Band of the hand
Band of the hand
Band of the hand
Band of the hand

Listen to me Mr. Pusherman
This might be your last night in a bed so soft
There are pimps on the make, politicians on the take
You can't pay us off

We're gonna blow up your home of Voodoo
And watch it burn without any regret
We got the power, we're the new government

五指成拳，五人成团

黑鬼们和白鬼们
窃取了小子们的性命
财富是一件污秽的衣服
如此色情如此不爱国
如此包裹在星条旗中

作妖的人渣盘剥着哑巴
把孩儿们都唆使成骗子和奴隶
把死抽死嗑的毒贩当英雄和神人
这帮东西都该被送进坟墓

五指成拳，五人成团
五指成拳，五人成团
五指成拳，五人成团
五指成拳，五人成团

听我说大毒枭先生
这也许是你在床上安寝的最后一夜
皮条客们谋财，政客们贪腐
可你无法收买我们

我们要炸掉你的巫毒老巢
全无遗憾看它烧掉
我们有权力，我们是新政府

You just don't know it yet

Band of the hand
Band of the hand
Band of the hand
Band of the hand

For all of my brothers from Vietnam
And my uncles from World War II
I've got to say that it's countdown time now
We're gonna do what the law should do

And for you pretty baby
I know your story is too painful to share
One day though you'll be talking in your sleep
And when you do, I wanna be there

Band of the hand
Band of the hand
Band of the hand
Band of the hand

你只是还不知道

五指成拳，五人成团
五指成拳，五人成团
五指成拳，五人成团
五指成拳，五人成团

为了我从越南回来的所有兄弟
还有从二战回来的叔伯
我得说现在开始倒计时了
我们要做原本法律做的事

也为了你啊漂亮宝贝
我知道你的故事苦不堪言
但有一天你会在梦中说起
当你这样做时，我想我要在那里

五指成拳，五人成团
五指成拳，五人成团
五指成拳，五人成团
五指成拳，五人成团

# *DOWN IN THE GROOVE*
# 妙境深处

死亡不是终结

做了个关于你的梦，宝贝

附加歌词

一夜又一夜

the priest wore black on the 7th day tilted
And waltzed across a sloping floor waltz
What I'd begun, you couldn't finish
And tilted his hat to me false
You could [You thought she was a party doll
(You fell for) Her personality and I was I was
just along for the ride
A houndog . . . as I was for I'd just met her at the
That's not the way it happened, Mister Red X
I thought you were someone else Store
IT MUST'VE BEEN THE MASK YOU WORE
I figured (I supposed) I've lost you anyway
— for the five
There would be just your voice & mine
(trying to touch each other a wave your face
You must think I'm someone else / I never saw your (it must've been because you
I hadn't called you for days & days, it wasn't because were hard to
you were hard to reach
I knew what we were going to say
(Creeping across the rooftops, jumping but I hadn't memorized my (goodbye)
part of the speech
I figured I lost you anyway
So I pulled up stakes and went for broke
It didn't strike me very funny I focused
focus the cats had
We didn't speak for days & days, it must've been got our tongue
They put me on a pedestal
Filled me up with beans and coke
And I figured I lost you anyway And when I lost you
it all came clear
And then you thought it all a joke that to
But it didn't strike me very funny
I thought you were hypnotized but you thought it was sinister
So For I figured I lost you anyway I was
So what be the use I imagine & you were loose
In order to get time to you, I'd just have to
I'd have to use some excuse I come up with some
excuse
It was funny (It just struck me kind of funny)
I didn't call you for days & days and, it wasn't cause
cat had my tongue
(We hadn't talked for got
I didn't talk for days & days and, it wasn't cause the cat
had got my tongue
It was just that every key I said was and when the rains came, the
We didn't talk for days & days words were
It Ain't my fault nobody ever took the time to teach me gone
taught me how to forgive
Bletherers take me for a fool

After you came down on me, you said you
never saw
my face before

《妙境深处》是迪伦的第 25 张录音室专辑，由哥伦比亚唱片公司于 1988 年 5 月 30 日发行，受到评论界一致的负面评价。

专辑在曲目选择上几经反复，合作乐手纷杂，制作时间长达 6 年。10 首歌曲中，有 2 首迪伦原创作品，2 首迪伦作曲、罗伯特·亨特（Robert Hunter）作词的作品，1 首迪伦改编的 19 世纪美国民歌，5 首翻唱歌曲。[1]

评论界普遍认为，这是迪伦水准线以下的专辑。2007 年，《滚石》杂志将其列为迪伦最差专辑。该杂志 2017 年补充道："迪伦的歌迷永远都会争论迪伦的职业生涯跌入谷底的确切时刻，但大多数人都将其确定为 1988 年 5 月，《妙境深处》'轰'地登临唱片店的那一刻。"

2 首迪伦原创作品：《做了个关于你的梦，宝贝》，"回收"自电影《火之心》（*Hearts of Fire*）插曲；《死亡不是终结》则是迪伦 1983 年专辑《异教徒》的弃用之作。本书中，另收入电影《火之心》另一首插曲《一夜又一夜》。

1986 年 8 月，迪伦参与了英国导演理查德·马昆德

[1] 本书仅收录其中 2 首歌曲及 1 首附加歌词。——编者注

（Richard Marquand）的音乐剧情片《火之心》的拍摄，在片中担任主演并为电影撰写歌曲。这种安排，显见有一部分原因是想要借助迪伦的名气。但电影上映后反响不佳。1987 年在英国首映，2 周后就被迫下线。在美国则是“1 周游”，只在极少数影院上映。

迪伦为电影所作的 2 首插曲，不同于他之前情歌的个性面貌。《做了个关于你的梦，宝贝》通俗而浅近，像是大众普通情歌；《一夜又一夜》也是这样，只是更糟，似乎是草草写就、仓促收场。

《火之心》折射了 20 世纪 80 年代的空虚，人们跃上娱乐生活的表面，似乎是空心的。迪伦也失去了神采。1987 年 9 月 4 日，电影上映后不久，50 岁的马昆德导演因中风不治去世。

《妙境深处》，实际上是低谷深处，此时迪伦正经历灵感缺失、才尽灯枯的低迷期。就算是翻唱，除了《时速 90 码（冲向断头路）》［“Ninety Miles an Hour（Down a Dead End Street）”］等个别歌曲，都缺少他在其他时期翻唱他人作品时神魂俱在的饱满。全专辑只有可怜的 32 分 04 秒，与此对应，大多数翻唱都给人还没开始即忽然结束的短促感。

然而，联系到以后还会出现的翻唱专辑，以下方面值得注意：迪伦的非原创专辑，往往能够展示这位歌手、歌曲作家和诗人的来历，呈现出他在希宾长大期间给他以触动、为他打开广阔艺术世界的歌曲脉络。《妙境深处》的翻唱曲目从任何角度看都没有系统性，显示了迪伦不寻常的成长路径，对这些歌曲的回顾，有助于将迪伦从日益枯萎的感知力和可能正在固化的个人创作中拉出来，引向新的素材和创意。它确实是过渡性的，但对于一个永不停息、一直在成长的巨匠型人物，这种向后的徘徊是必要的，其结果也是积极的。

《死亡不是终结》是该专辑一个亮点，虽说歌词落在纸面上平平无奇，似乎全篇都是大话，但它面向所有人，讲的是人人都能切的题、个个都可感的话。它在大俗之中，迎向更加广阔的大众，可以作用于更多人。并且，在它响起的一刻你能感觉到，这是一个有神魂的时刻。

《死亡不是终结》的诞生，要往前回溯 3 张专辑，直至 1983 年。这首歌后来被不少知名歌手翻唱，大有从黑暗的最低点、从绝处跃起的信心。

《妙境深处》经历了纽约、伦敦和好莱坞的 3 个录音室，涉及 30 多位音乐人，从 1983 年 5 月 2 日，经过 5 个年头、至少 14 场录音，至 1987 年 6 月 23 日才录制完成。

又犹豫、修改了近一年，这张专辑才发行。紧随其后，迪伦开始巡演。这回的巡演有一个重大转变：伴奏团队从群星荟萃、规模宏大的乐团，转为小型的车库摇滚乐队。曲目选择也变得落拓不羁，不同场次都不一样。迪伦有时用全乐队，有时用电声组合，有时用更小型的原声组合。正是在原声组合的表演中，迪伦汇入了仿佛无穷无尽的各种传统歌曲的翻唱。

音乐会起初没受到多少关注，但随着迪伦的坚持，几年后声名鹊起。对于迪伦这个年纪来说，巡演日程密集得令人惊讶——他大部分时间都在路上，一站结束，很快投入下一站。这个“永不停止的巡演（Never Ending Tour）”，从 1988 年夏天开始，一直延续至今天。

## DEATH IS NOT THE END

When you're sad and when you're lonely
And you haven't got a friend
Just remember that death is not the end
And all that you've held sacred
Falls down and does not mend
Just remember that death is not the end
Not the end, not the end
Just remember that death is not the end

When you're standing at the crossroads
That you cannot comprehend
Just remember that death is not the end
And all your dreams have vanished
And you don't know what's up the bend
Just remember that death is not the end
Not the end, not the end
Just remember that death is not the end

When the storm clouds gather 'round you
And heavy rains descend

## 死亡不是终结[1]

当你又悲哀又孤独
连一个朋友都没有
记住吧死亡不是终结
当你认为神圣的一切
坍塌下来，无可挽救
记住吧死亡不是终结
不是终结，不是终结
请记住死亡不是终结

当你站在十字路口
心中茫然无解
记住吧死亡不是终结
而你所有的梦都破灭了
不知道弯道后会是什么
记住吧死亡不是终结
不是终结，不是终结
请记住死亡不是终结

当乌云集于你四周
暴雨倾盆而下

---

[1] 这一辑均由郝佳校译。

Just remember that death is not the end
And there's no one there to comfort you
With a helpin' hand to lend
Just remember that death is not the end
Not the end, not the end
Just remember that death is not the end

Oh, the tree of life is growing
Where the spirit never dies
And the bright light of salvation shines
In dark and empty skies

When the cities are on fire
With the burning flesh of men
Just remember that death is not the end
And you search in vain to find
Just one law-abiding citizen
Just remember that death is not the end
Not the end, not the end
Just remember that death is not the end

记住吧死亡不是终结
而没有人施以援手
给你慰藉
记住吧死亡不是终结
不是终结，不是终结
请记住死亡不是终结

啊，生命之树常青
于灵魂永存之地
救赎之明光闪耀
在黑暗虚无的天际

当城市全烧起来
烧灼着人的肉身
记住吧死亡不是终结
而你四处搜寻
也难找到一个守法公民
记住吧死亡不是终结
不是终结，不是终结
请记住死亡不是终结

## HAD A DREAM ABOUT YOU, BABY

I got to see you baby, I don't care
It may be someplace, baby, you say where

I had a dream about you, baby
Had a dream about you, baby
Late last night you come a-rollin' across my mind

You got the crazy rhythm when you walk
You make me nervous when you start to talk

I had a dream about you, baby
Had a dream about you, baby
Late last night you come a-rollin' across my mind

Standin' on the highway, you flag me down
Said, take me Daddy, to the nearest town

I had a dream about you, baby
Had a dream about you, baby
Late last night you come a-rollin' across my mind

The joint is jumpin'

## 做了个关于你的梦，宝贝

我要见你宝贝，我不管
在什么地方，宝贝，你说了算

我做了个关于你的梦，宝贝
做了个关于你的梦，宝贝
昨天深夜你旋转着，掠过我的心头

你一迈步就带来一股疯狂的节奏
你一开口我就紧张万分

我做了个关于你的梦，宝贝
做了个关于你的梦，宝贝
昨天深夜你旋转着，掠过我的心头

站在公路上，你打手势让我停下
说带我一程大叔，去最近的镇子

我做了个关于你的梦，宝贝
做了个关于你的梦，宝贝
昨天深夜你旋转着，掠过我的心头

关节在跳跃

It's really somethin'
The beat is pumpin'
My heart is thumpin'
Spent my money on you honey
My limbs are shakin'
My heart is breakin'

You kiss me, baby, in the coffee shop
You make me nervous, you gotta stop

I had a dream about you, baby
Had a dream about you, baby
Late last night you come a-rollin' across my mind

You got a rag wrapped around your head
Wearing a long dress fire engine red

I had a dream about you, baby
Had a dream about you, baby
Late last night you come a-rollin' across my mind

这实在太奇妙
脉搏在加速
心脏扑扑跳
给你花了钱啊小宝贝
我的手脚乱摇
我的心就要爆

你吻我，宝贝，在咖啡店里
你让我紧张万分，你得停下

我做了个关于你的梦，宝贝
做了个关于你的梦，宝贝
昨天深夜你旋转着，掠过我的心头

你用一块破布包着头
穿的长裙是消防车的红色

我做了个关于你的梦，宝贝
做了个关于你的梦，宝贝
昨天深夜你旋转着，掠过我的心头

## NIGHT AFTER NIGHT

Night after night you wander the streets of my mind
Night after night don't know what you think you will find
No place to go, nowhere to turn
Everything around you seems to burn, burn, burn
And there's never any mercy in sight night after night

Night after night
Night after night

Night after night some new plan to blow up the world
Night after night another old man kissing some young girl
You look for salvation, you find none
Just another broken heart, another barrel of a gun
Just another stick of dynamite night after night

Night after night
Night after night

Night after night you drop dead in your bed
Night after night another bottle finds a head
Night after night I think about cutting you loose
But I just can't do it, what would be the use?

## 一夜又一夜

一夜又一夜你漫游在我心灵的街
一夜又一夜不知道你以为你会发现什么
无路可走，无处可逃
你周围的一切似乎都在燃烧，燃烧，燃烧
一直都看不到任何悲悯一夜又一夜

一夜又一夜
一夜又一夜

一夜又一夜新的引爆世界的设想
一夜又一夜又一个糟老头吻着某位小姑娘
你寻找着拯救，什么都没找见
只找到又一颗破碎的心，又一支枪管
只找到又一管炸药一夜又一夜

一夜又一夜
一夜又一夜

一夜又一夜你像死人倒在床上
一夜又一夜又一瓶酒找到宿醉一场
一夜又一夜我考虑着要让你解脱
可我就是做不到，那有什么用呢？

So I just keep a-holding you tight night after night

Night after night

Night after night

所以我只能将你抱紧一夜又一夜

一夜又一夜
一夜又一夜

# *OH MERCY*
# 哦，慈悲

政治世界

泪珠滚落之地

一切皆已破碎

把钟敲响吧

穿黑长衣的男人

多数时候

我有何用？

狂妄症

你想要什么？

流星

**附加歌词**

一连串梦

尊严

You were always thinking about her
But she slipped away and you lost her trail
And now that you can't do without her
She's back in town like a nightingale
And there ain't gonna be any next time
By now you better understand
That there ain't gonna be any next time
So hold her and kiss her and love her while you can
- - - - - - - - - - - - -

迪伦在自传中透露，1987 年，一次偶然的事故使他的一只手受到重创，皮开肉绽，打上了石膏，原计划的 100 多场演出成了泡影，他却也因此有了一段自省的经历。“在此之前，我一直在欺骗自己，我对于自身才华的运用已远远超出了其本身的限度。”他还反省说，“我踯躅在人行道上。在我身上，有一个人找不到了，我需要找到他。”[1]

迪伦已有许久不主动创作，他感觉一段时间以来，录制唱片一直很难。“作品很多但从不准确，让人分心的事情太多，结果我的音乐道路变成了藤蔓缠绕的丛林。我一直在遵循旧有的习俗，但现在它们不起作用了。”[2]

在什么都不能做的情况下，一天晚上，家人都睡了，迪伦坐在厨房的桌子旁，山坡上除了月光什么都没有，什么都变了。一首歌词不请自来，迪伦把它叫作《政治世界》。之后的一个月，迪伦又陆续写了 20 首。“它们来源于我抑郁的心情。如果我不是伤病如此，也许我无法写下它们。”

---

[1] [美]鲍勃·迪伦. 像一块滚石：鲍勃·迪伦回忆录（第一卷）[M]. 徐振锋，吴宏凯，译. 南京：江苏人民出版社，2006.

[2] 同上。

在U2乐队主唱波诺（Bono）的牵线下，1989年2月，迪伦开始与加拿大制作人丹尼尔·拉努瓦（Daniel Lanois）合作，制作他的第26张录音室专辑，并于1989年9月12日，由哥伦比亚唱片公司发行。

《哦，慈悲》的录制，借助于拉努瓦发明的"即拿即走"录音室，假座新奥尔良一座维多利亚风格的宅邸进行。从1989年2月底到7月初，4个多月时间里，录制加叠录，共进行了30多场录音。

迪伦定了一个规则，只在晚上录。拉努瓦理解，身体在夜晚有一种节奏，与月潮有关。以致在夜晚，我们会变得更加神秘和黑暗。结果就是，《哦，慈悲》成为一张适合在晚上听的唱片。"是两个人待在后门廊的那种气氛。"所有歌曲都是谦逊而优美的，"其中的三四首，听起来就像深夜广播或大洪水之后的歌曲。"（罗伯特·克里斯戈语）

这张专辑驱散了那些对迪伦创作力的质疑，带着近乎正统的文学性，散发着诗性的光辉。尽管歌曲主旨仍是迪伦本色，但它们的视角和状态都变了，与其他专辑不同。前所未有的，迪伦处于游离于自身之外的状态，仿佛灵魂已经出窍，在神秘的朦胧夜色中，飘荡在人间万物之间。头一次，迪伦对他所感念的对象不是直接批评，也不是自感自受，虽然批评和感受只会更多，但这是一种沉潜的、内在的、笼统的、静观的、更似上帝的视角。迪伦对《流星》的自识，似可用来形容这所有的歌曲，"它既冷淡又热烈，充满了渴望——孤独，疏远。有很多痛苦藏在里面”。[1]

《政治世界》当然是由现实事件引发的，一场激烈的总统竞选正进行得如火如荼，但“歌里的‘政治世界’更像地狱，而非我们在其中生活、辛劳和死亡的世界”。《我有何用？》来源于迪伦在街上所见，一位警察在喝令无家可归的流浪汉离开，但它试图抓住一种更悲凉的无能，而不仅仅是指涉具体事件。《尊严》和《狂妄症》都来自新闻，但它不是“拿手电筒去照人的脸”，迪伦自己解释说，“在这样的一首歌里，事物没有尽头”，“直到我能够读懂其精神实质，这首歌才能真正产生”。《一切皆已破碎》不是自传性的，“但它来自一个自传性的地方”。《多数时候》像是迪伦的另一个自我。《把钟敲响吧》灵感源于《马太福音》——迪伦的末日信念。《流星》是在新奥尔良写下的新曲，“当你的头脑非常清醒，能看到和感觉到事物，但你身体别的部分却在沉睡时，你就会听到这种歌。”《泪珠滚落之地》“很像是一个人拉着绳子去阻止火车”，富有魔力。《穿黑长衣的男人》来自深渊、这个星球上最神秘的地方，属于大师写出的锐利歌词，能击中人身上最脆弱的部位。

《哦，慈悲》是一张“声音魔术师打造的唱片”。迪伦说：“我最喜欢拉努瓦的一点是，他不想仅仅停留在事情的表面。他甚至不想游泳。他喜欢跳进去，潜入水底。他想娶一条美人鱼。”这场伟大歌手与杰出艺匠的神交磕磕绊绊，甚至有时濒临崩盘，但是他们把这事儿做成了。

---

[1] [美]鲍勃·迪伦.像一块滚石：鲍勃·迪伦回忆录(第一卷)[M].徐振锋，吴宏凯，译.南京：江苏人民出版社，2006.

## POLITICAL WORLD

We live in a political world
Love don't have any place
We're living in times where men commit crimes
And crime don't have a face

We live in a political world
Icicles hanging down
Wedding bells ring and angels sing
Clouds cover up the ground

We live in a political world
Wisdom is thrown into jail
It rots in a cell, is misguided as hell
Leaving no one to pick up a trail

We live in a political world
Where mercy walks the plank
Life is in mirrors, death disappears
Up the steps into the nearest bank

## 政治世界[1]

我们生活在一个政治世界
爱没有位置
我们生活在人人犯罪的时代
罪行没有面目

我们生活在一个政治世界
冰挂自上垂下
婚礼钟声敲响，天使歌唱
重云遮住大地

我们生活在一个政治世界
智慧锒铛入狱
它在号子里腐烂，被认为是狗屎
让任何人都不能觅其踪迹

我们生活在一个政治世界
这里仁慈走跳板[2]
生命在镜中，死亡失踪
拾级而上就是最近的银行

---

[1] 本篇由杨盈盈校译。
[2] 走跳板，海盗处死俘虏的一种方式。

We live in a political world
Where courage is a thing of the past
Houses are haunted, children are unwanted
The next day could be your last

We live in a political world
The one we can see and can feel
But there's no one to check, it's all a stacked deck
We all know for sure that it's real

We live in a political world
In the cities of lonesome fear
Little by little you turn in the middle
But you're never sure why you're here

We live in a political world
Under the microscope
You can travel anywhere and hang yourself there
You always got more than enough rope

We live in a political world
Turning and a-thrashing about
As soon as you're awake, you're trained to take
What looks like the easy way out

我们生活在一个政治世界
这里勇气已是陈年旧事
房子在闹鬼，孩子们没人要
明天就可能是你的末日

我们生活在一个政治世界
这就是看得见和摸得着的
但没人去核检，它只是张作弊纸牌
无疑我们都知道，这是真的

我们生活在一个政治世界
在孤独恐惧的一座座城
一点一点你在中途转向
为何你在这儿，这你永远搞不懂

我们生活在一个政治世界
生活在显微镜底
你可以随便找个地方上吊
你总能弄到绰绰有余的绳子

我们生活在一个政治世界
你翻来又覆去
一旦醒来，就会受训
接受看似简单的出路

We live in a political world
Where peace is not welcome at all
It's turned away from the door to wander some more
Or put up against the wall

We live in a political world
Everything is hers or his
Climb into the frame and shout God's name
But you're never sure what it is

我们生活在一个政治世界
和平不受欢迎
它要么被拒门外继续徘徊
要么就冲墙待着

我们生活在一个政治世界
一切都是她的或他的
爬进画框高呼上帝之名
但你永远不确定这是什么事

## WHERE TEARDROPS FALL

Far away where the soft winds blow
Far away from it all
There is a place you go
Where teardrops fall

Far away in the stormy night
Far away and over the wall
You are there in the flickering light
Where teardrops fall

We banged the drum slowly
And played the fife lowly
You know the song in my heart
In the turning of twilight
In the shadows of moonlight
You can show me a new place to start

I've torn my clothes and I've drained the cup
Strippin' away at it all
Thinking of you when the sun comes up
Where teardrops fall

## 泪珠滚落之地

远方微风徐徐
远方飞离一切
那儿有你欲往之所
在泪珠滚落之地

远方风雨如晦
远方飞越这铁壁
你在别处，在闪烁灯火里
在泪珠滚落之地

我们缓缓击鼓
我们低低奏笛
你知晓我心中歌曲
在黄昏转接处
在月色光影里
你指给我新开始

我撕开衣裳，饮干了酒
弃绝一切
在太阳升起时想你
在泪珠滚落之地

By rivers of blindness
In love and with kindness
We could hold up a toast if we meet
To the cuttin' of fences
To sharpen the senses
That linger in the fireball heat

Roses are red, violets are blue
And time is beginning to crawl
I just might have to come see you
Where teardrops fall

在失明河川边
在爱意中，怀着友善
相会时我们可以举杯相庆
为劈开了藩篱
为留在火球炽热中的感官
变得锐敏

玫瑰红红，紫罗兰幽蓝
而时光开始慢慢前行
可能我一定会来见你
在泪珠滚落之地

## EVERYTHING IS BROKEN

Broken lines, broken strings
Broken threads, broken springs
Broken idols, broken heads
People sleeping in broken beds
Ain't no use jiving, ain't no use joking
Everything is broken

Broken bottles, broken plates
Broken switches, broken gates
Broken dishes, broken parts
Streets are filled with broken hearts
Broken words never meant to be spoken
Everything is broken

Seem like every time you stop and turn around
Something else just hit the ground

Broken cutters, broken saws
Broken buckles, broken laws
Broken bodies, broken bones
Broken voices on broken phones
Take a deep breath, feel like you're chokin'

## 一切皆已破碎

破碎的线，破碎的弦
破碎的螺纹，破碎的弹簧
破碎的偶像，破碎的头
人睡在破碎的床上
哄骗没用，玩笑没用
一切皆已破碎

破碎的瓶，破碎的盘
破碎的开关，破碎的门板
破碎的碗碟，破碎的零件
满街都是破碎的心
破碎的言语永远不该说出口
一切皆已破碎

好像你每次停下转身
都有东西刚刚落在地上

破碎的刀具，破碎的钢锯
破碎的搭扣，破碎的法律
破碎的肉身，破碎的骨骼
破碎的电话里破碎的声音
深吸一口气，感觉快要窒息

Everything is broken

Every time you leave and go off someplace
Things fall to pieces in my face

Broken hands on broken ploughs
Broken treaties, broken vows
Broken pipes, broken tools
People bending broken rules
Hound dog howling, bullfrog croaking
Everything is broken

一切皆已破碎

每次你离开去往他方
万物就碎落在我脸上

破碎的手握着破碎的犁
破碎的协议，破碎的誓词
破碎的管道，破碎的工具
人屈从于破碎的规矩
猎犬吠叫，牛蛙鼓噪
一切皆已破碎

## RING THEM BELLS

Ring them bells, ye heathen
From the city that dreams
Ring them bells from the sanctuaries
'Cross the valleys and streams
For they're deep and they're wide
And the world's on its side
And time is running backwards
And so is the bride

Ring them bells St. Peter
Where the four winds blow
Ring them bells with an iron hand
So the people will know
Oh it's rush hour now
On the wheel and the plow
And the sun is going down
Upon the sacred cow

Ring them bells Sweet Martha
For the poor man's son

# 把钟敲响吧[1]

把钟敲响吧，你们
来自昏睡之城的异教徒
自避难所把钟敲响吧
让它穿过山谷和江河
因为山谷幽深，江河宽广
世界就在两旁
时光在向后奔跑
新娘也是这样

把钟敲响吧圣彼得
在四风鼓荡之地
用铁腕把钟敲响吧
由此人们将获悉
哦高峰已至
他们赶着车，负着犁
而太阳伏在圣牛背上
往前走下去

把钟敲响吧可爱的马大
为那个穷人家的小伙

[1] 本篇由杨盈盈校译。

Ring them bells so the world will know
That God is one
Oh the shepherd is asleep
Where the willows weep
And the mountains are filled
With lost sheep

Ring them bells for the blind and the deaf
Ring them bells for all of us who are left
Ring them bells for the chosen few
Who will judge the many when the game is through
Ring them bells, for the time that flies
For the child that cries
When innocence dies

Ring them bells St. Catherine
From the top of the room
Ring them from the fortress
For the lilies that bloom
Oh the lines are long
And the fighting is strong
And they're breaking down the distance
Between right and wrong

把钟敲响，由此世界将明白
神只有一个
哦牧羊人睡了
在杨柳低泣的地方
漫山遍野都是
迷途的羔羊

把钟敲响，为盲人和聋人
把钟敲响，为我们这些被留下的
把钟敲响，为被拣选的少数
他们将审判众人，当游戏结束
把钟敲响吧，为飞驰的光阴
为纯真死去时
那哭泣的孩子

把钟敲响吧圣凯瑟琳[1]
从那间房的屋顶
从城堡开始敲响
为盛开的百合而鸣
哦队伍漫长
战斗激烈
而钟声消去了
对与错的距离

---

[1] 圣凯瑟琳，据传她去拜访罗马皇帝马克森提乌斯，劝其勿迫害基督徒，被杀害。

## MAN IN THE LONG BLACK COAT

Crickets are chirpin', the water is high
There's a soft cotton dress on the line hangin' dry
Window wide open, African trees
Bent over backwards from a hurricane breeze
Not a word of goodbye, not even a note
She gone with the man
In the long black coat

Somebody seen him hanging around
At the old dance hall on the outskirts of town
He looked into her eyes when she stopped him to ask
If he wanted to dance, he had a face like a mask
Somebody said from the Bible he'd quote
There was dust on the man
In the long black coat

The preacher was a-talkin', there's a sermon he gave
He said, "Every man's conscience is vile and depraved
You cannot depend on it to be your guide
When it's you who must keep it satisfied."
It ain't easy to swallow, it sticks in the throat
She gave her heart to the man

## 穿黑长衣的男人

蟋蟀长鸣，河水高涨
一件柔软的棉布裙晾在衣绳上
窗子大开，非洲的树
俯身朝向飓风相反的方向
无一声道别，甚至没张纸条
她走了
跟那个穿黑长衣的男人

有人在城郊老舞厅看见他
一个人晃来晃去
她拦下他问，要不要跳支舞
他端详她的眼，他有一张像面具的脸
有人用他援引过的《圣经》说
穿黑长衣的男人
身上尽是风尘

牧师在讲话，他正在布道
他说 :“人的天良已经卑污堕落
切切不可仰赖它作引导
当你必须去满足它。”
这话不易接受，如鲠在喉
她把心交给了那个

In the long black coat

There are no mistakes in life some people say
And it's true sometimes you can see it that way
I went down to the river but I just missed the boat
She went with the man
In the long black coat

There's smoke on the water, it's been there since June
Tree trunks uprooted, 'neath the high crescent moon
Feel the pulse and vibration and the rumbling force
Somebody is out there beating on a dead horse
She never said nothing, there was nothing she wrote
She went with the man
In the long black coat

## 穿黑长衣的男人

人生没有错误，有人说
的确，有时候你可以那样看
我一路赶到河边，却还是误了船
她走了
跟那个穿黑长衣的男人

水面上笼着烟，六月以来便如此
高高的新月下，树木被连根拔起
感受这脉搏、颤动和隆隆之力
有人在那里拍打一匹死马
她从不说话，也没写过什么
她走了
跟那个穿黑长衣的男人

## MOST OF THE TIME

Most of the time
I'm clear focused all around
Most of the time
I can keep both feet on the ground
I can follow the path, I can read the signs
Stay right with it when the road unwinds
I can handle whatever I stumble upon
I don't even notice she's gone
Most of the time

Most of the time
It's well understood
Most of the time
I wouldn't change it if I could
I can make it all match up, I can hold my own
I can deal with the situation right down to the bone
I can survive, I can endure
And I don't even think about her
Most of the time

Most of the time
My head is on straight

## 多数时候

多数时候
我全神贯注
多数时候
我能脚踏实地
我会循路前行，辨清路牌标识
当道路畅达，我也便保持正确
不管遭遇如何我都能应付
甚至没注意到她已离去
多数时候

多数时候
事情显而易见
多数时候
如果可以的话我不会改变
我能让事事妥帖，能守住自我
能直入核心解决问题
我能绝处逢生，能隐忍
甚至都不再惦念她
多数时候

多数时候
我头脑清醒

Most of the time
I'm strong enough not to hate
I don't build up illusion 'til it makes me sick
I ain't afraid of confusion no matter how thick
I can smile in the face of mankind
Don't even remember what her lips felt like on mine
Most of the time

Most of the time
She ain't even in my mind
I wouldn't know her if I saw her
She's that far behind
Most of the time
I can't even be sure
If she was ever with me
Or if I was with her

Most of the time
I'm halfway content
Most of the time
I know exactly where it went
I don't cheat on myself, I don't run and hide
Hide from the feelings that are buried inside
I don't compromise and I don't pretend
I don't even care if I ever see her again
Most of the time

多数时候
我足够强大不致怨恨
幻想不生直到这让我恶心
不惧困惑不管这多严重
我会对人面带微笑
甚至记不起她的唇在我唇上的感觉
多数时候

多数时候
她甚至不在我心间
就算见到她我也不认识
她已那么遥远
多数时候
我甚至不能确定
是否她跟我有过一段
或我跟她有过一段

多数时候
我过得马马虎虎
多数时候
我完全明白去向何处
我不自欺，不逃避
不回避埋在内心的情感
我不妥协也不假装
甚至不在意能否和她再见
多数时候

## WHAT GOOD AM I?

What good am I if I'm like all the rest
If I just turn away, when I see how you're dressed
If I shut myself off so I can't hear you cry
What good am I?

What good am I if I know and don't do
If I see and don't say, if I look right through you
If I turn a deaf ear to the thunderin' sky
What good am I?

What good am I while you softly weep
And I hear in my head what you say in your sleep
And I freeze in the moment like the rest who don't try
What good am I?

What good am I then to others and me
If I've had every chance and yet still fail to see
If my hands are tied must I not wonder within
Who tied them and why and where must I have been?

What good am I if I say foolish things
And I laugh in the face of what sorrow brings

## 我有何用？

我有何用如果我像他人一般
看见你的衣着，就别过脸
如果我封闭自己就为听不见你叫喊
我有何用？

我有何用如果我知道却做不到
看见却不说穿，一双眼总是透过你视而不见
如果我将一只聋耳对着震天的雷鸣
我有何用？

我有何用当你低低哀泣
我脑中听到的却是你梦中的呓语
而我就冻结在那一刻就像其他看客
我有何用？

我有何用于人于己
如果我坐拥每个机会却仍未洞悉
如果我双手被缚难道内心不该怀疑
是谁绑了我、为什么、我这时该去哪里？

我有何用如果我一派胡言
还笑那哀戚的脸

And I just turn my back while you silently die

What good am I?

还在你默默死去时背过身去

我有何用?

## DISEASE OF CONCEIT

There's a whole lot of people suffering tonight
From the disease of conceit
Whole lot of people struggling tonight
From the disease of conceit
Comes right down the highway
Straight down the line
Rips into your senses
Through your body and your mind
Nothing about it that's sweet
The disease of conceit

There's a whole lot of hearts breaking tonight
From the disease of conceit
Whole lot of hearts shaking tonight
From the disease of conceit
Steps into your room
Eats your soul
Over your senses
You have no control
Ain't nothing too discreet
About the disease of conceit

## 狂妄症

今夜许多人在受苦
因这狂妄症
今夜许多人在挣扎
因这狂妄症
沿高速公路俯冲
径直沿着线
撕开你的感官
突入你的身体和大脑
没什么好说的
这狂妄症

今夜许多心在迸裂
因这狂妄症
今夜许多心在颤抖
因这狂妄症
跨进你的门
吞掉你的魂
压倒你的理智
你失去控制
再无一丝审慎
对这狂妄症

There's a whole lot of people dying tonight
From the disease of conceit
Whole lot of people crying tonight
From the disease of conceit
Comes right out of nowhere
And you're down for the count
From the outside world
The pressure will mount
Turn you into a piece of meat
The disease of conceit

Conceit is a disease
That the doctors got no cure
They've done a lot of research on it
But what it is, they're still not sure

There's a whole lot of people in trouble tonight
From the disease of conceit
Whole lot of people seeing double tonight
From the disease of conceit
Give ya delusions of grandeur
And a evil eye
Give you the idea that
You're too good to die
Then they bury you from your head to your feet
From the disease of conceit

今夜许多人奄奄一息
因这狂妄症
今夜许多人大喊大叫
因这狂妄症
它从无明中骤现
你在倒数中倒下
这外部世界
压力陡升
将把你压成肉饼
这狂妄症

狂妄是一种病
医生无能为力
他们做了很多研究
可这病是什么，仍不确定

今夜许多人危机重重
因这狂妄症
今夜许多人眼见那重影
因这狂妄症
给了你伟大的妄念
以及一只恶眼
让你以为
你好得不会死亡
然后它就把你从头到脚埋葬
用这狂妄症

## WHAT WAS IT YOU WANTED?

What was it you wanted?
Tell me again so I'll know
What's happening in there
What's going on in your show
What was it you wanted
Could you say it again?
I'll be back in a minute
You can get it together by then

What was it you wanted
You can tell me, I'm back
We can start it all over
Get it back on the track
You got my attention
Go ahead, speak
What was it you wanted
When you were kissing my cheek?

Was there somebody looking
When you give me that kiss
Someone there in the shadows
Someone that I might have missed?

## 你想要什么？

你想要什么？
再说一遍让我明白
你那儿发生了什么
你节目中发生了什么
你想要什么
能再说一遍吗？
我一会儿就回来
到时你可以一起说

你想要什么？
讲给我听，我回来了
咱从头开始
回到正题
我在注意听你说
说吧，继续
你想要什么
当你亲我脸的时候？

有人在看吗
当你给了我那个吻
某个在暗处的人
某个我可能没注意的人？

Is there something you needed
Something I don't understand
What was it you wanted
Do I have it here in my hand?

Whatever you wanted
Slipped out of my mind
Would you remind me again
If you'd be so kind
Has the record been breaking
Did the needle just skip
Is there somebody waiting
Was there a slip of the lip?

What was it you wanted
I ain't keeping score
Are you the same person
That was here before?
Is it something important?
Maybe not
What was it you wanted?
Tell me again I forgot

Whatever you wanted
What could it be
Did somebody tell you

有你要的东西吗
某种我不理解的东西
你想要什么
我手里头有吗?

不管你想要的是什么
都已从我脑中划过
你能再提醒我一下吗
如果你能发发好心
是唱片坏了吗
刚才跳针了吗
是有什么人在等吗
有什么说漏嘴吗?

你想要什么?
我已了无头绪
你和之前在这儿的
是同一个人吗?
那事情重要吗?
也许不重要
你想要什么?
再说一遍吧，我忘了

无论你想要什么
那会是什么呢
有人告诉你

That you could get it from me
Is it something that comes natural
Is it easy to say
Why do you want it
Who are you anyway?

Is the scenery changing
Am I getting it wrong
Is the whole thing going backwards
Are they playing our song?
Where were you when it started
Do you want it for free
What was it you wanted
Are you talking to me?

你能从我这儿得到吗
那自然而然吗
说起来容易吗
你为什么想要它
你到底是谁?

布景在变换吗
是我搞错了吗
整件事都在往回倒吗
他们在放我们的歌吗?
开始时你在哪儿?
你是想要免费的吗
你想要什么?
你在跟我说话吗?

## SHOOTING STAR

Seen a shooting star tonight
And I thought of you
You were trying to break into another world
A world I never knew
I always kind of wondered
If you ever made it through
Seen a shooting star tonight
And I thought of you

Seen a shooting star tonight
And I thought of me
If I was still the same
If I ever became what you wanted me to be
Did I miss the mark or overstep the line
That only you could see?
Seen a shooting star tonight
And I thought of me

Listen to the engine, listen to the bell
As the last fire truck from hell
Goes rolling by
All good people are praying

## 流星

今夜看见了一颗流星
于是我想到你
你试图闯入另一个世界
一个我从不知晓的世界
我一直有几分好奇
你穿越成功了吗
今夜看见了一颗流星
于是我想到你

今夜看见了一颗流星
于是我想到我
是否还是原来的我
是否我变成了你希望的
我脱靶了还是越线了
这只有你才看得见？
今夜看见了一颗流星
于是我想到我

听那引擎，听那钟声
当地狱来的最后一辆救火车
呼啸着开过
所有的好人都在祈祷

It's the last temptation, the last account

The last time you might hear the sermon on the mount

The last radio is playing

Seen a shooting star tonight

Slip away

Tomorrow will be

Another day

Guess it's too late to say the things to you

That you needed to hear me say

Seen a shooting star tonight

Slip away

这是最后的诱惑，最后的账目
最后一次你听见登山宝训
最后一次广播在播音

今夜看见了一颗流星
倏忽不见
明天将会是
又一天
要说这些你想听我说的事
想必已经太晚
今夜看见了一颗流星
倏忽不见

## SERIES OF DREAMS

I was thinking of a series of dreams
Where nothing comes up to the top
Everything stays down where it's wounded
And comes to a permanent stop
Wasn't thinking of anything specific
Like in a dream, when someone wakes up and screams
Nothing too very scientific
Just thinking of a series of dreams

Thinking of a series of dreams
Where the time and the tempo fly
And there's no exit in any direction
'Cept the one that you can't see with your eyes
Wasn't making any great connection
Wasn't falling for any intricate scheme
Nothing that would pass inspection
Just thinking of a series of dreams

Dreams where the umbrella is folded
Into the path you are hurled

## 一连串梦

我想着一连串梦
梦里的一切都不往顶部升
只往下沉，在那儿遭受重击
进入永恒的静止
并未确切地想到什么
就像在梦中，有人会醒来尖叫
也没什么太科学
不过是想到了一连串梦

想着一连串梦
梦里节拍和节奏飞驰
任何方向都没有出口
除了你眼睛看不见的那处
未做任何奇异联想
未沉溺于任何复杂算计
没什么经得起检验
不过是想到了一连串梦

梦境里雨伞收拢
收进你被抛入的小径

---

[1] 本篇由杨盈盈校译。

And the cards are no good that you're holding
Unless they're from another world

In one, numbers were burning
In another, I witnessed a crime
In one, I was running, and in another
All I seemed to be doing was climb
Wasn't looking for any special assistance
Not going to any great extremes
I'd already gone the distance
Just thinking of a series of dreams

你手上的牌百无一用
除非它们来自另一个世界

一个梦里，数字在燃烧
另一个梦里，我目击了一场罪行
一个梦里，我在跑，而另一个梦
我似乎一直在爬
不求任何特别辅助
也没走极端
我已走了很远
不过是想到了一连串梦

## DIGNITY

Fat man lookin' in a blade of steel
Thin man lookin' at his last meal
Hollow man lookin' in a cottonfield
For dignity

Wise man lookin' in a blade of grass
Young man lookin' in the shadows that pass
Poor man lookin' through painted glass
For dignity

Somebody got murdered on New Year's Eve
Somebody said dignity was the first to leave
I went into the city, went into the town
Went into the land of the midnight sun

Searchin' high, searchin' low
Searchin' everywhere I know
Askin' the cops wherever I go
Have you seen dignity?

## 尊严[1]

胖子望着一把钢刀
瘦子望着最后一餐
空心人望着一片棉田
在寻找尊严

智者望着一片草叶
青年望着经过的影子
穷人望穿彩绘玻璃
在寻找尊严

有人在跨年夜被杀
有人说尊严最先离去
我走进城市，走进小镇
走进午夜阳光之地

向上求索，向下求索
求索我知晓的每个角落
走到哪儿我都问警官
你可曾见过尊严？

---

[1] 本篇由杨盈盈校译。

Blind man breakin' out of a trance
Puts both his hands in the pockets of chance
Hopin' to find one circumstance
Of dignity

I went to the wedding of Mary Lou
She said, "I don't want nobody see me talkin' to you"
Said she could get killed if she told me what she knew
About dignity

I went down where the vultures feed
I would've gone deeper, but there wasn't any need
Heard the tongues of angels and the tongues of men
Wasn't any difference to me

Chilly wind sharp as a razor blade
House on fire, debts unpaid
Gonna stand at the window, gonna ask the maid
Have you seen dignity?

Drinkin' man listens to the voice he hears
In a crowded room full of covered-up mirrors
Lookin' into the lost forgotten years
For dignity

Met Prince Phillip at the home of the blues

盲人从恍惚中惊觉
将两手插入机运的口袋
希望找到一个
尊严的姿态

我去参加玛丽·卢的婚礼
她说："我不想让人看到我和你说话"
她说这会招来杀身之祸，若告诉我她知道的
关于尊严的事

我走入秃鹫猎食之所
我本可以进入更深，但没那个必要
听到天使的话和人的话
于我而言并无分别

寒风像刀锋般尖利
房子着火，负债未还
想去窗边站站，想问问女仆
你可曾见过尊严？

饮酒者侧耳听他听到的声音
在满是蒙尘镜子的拥挤房间
从已然丢失的遗忘岁月
寻找尊严

在蓝调之家遇见菲利普亲王

Said he'd give me information if his name wasn't used
He wanted money up front, said he was abused
By dignity

Footprints runnin' 'cross the silver sand
Steps goin' down into tattoo land
I met the sons of darkness and the sons of light
In the bordertowns of despair

Got no place to fade, got no coat
I'm on the rollin' river in a jerkin' boat
Tryin' to read a note somebody wrote
About dignity

Sick man lookin' for the doctor's cure
Lookin' at his hands for the lines that were
And into every masterpiece of literature
For dignity

Englishman stranded in the blackheart wind
Combin' his hair back, his future looks thin
Bites the bullet and he looks within
For dignity

Someone showed me a picture and I just laughed
Dignity never been photographed

说会给我信息只要不提他名字
他要求现金预付，说他被滥用了
被尊严这东西

脚印穿过银沙
脚步走进文身之地
我遇见黑暗之子和光明之子
在绝望的边境城市

找不到归隐处，找不到遮盖
我在滔滔江面，在颠簸的小船里
努力阅读一个人写的
关于尊严的笔记

病人在寻求医生的诊疗
看着自己的手读取掌纹
并进入每一部文学经典
寻找尊严

英国人被困于黑心风
头发梳向脑后，前景看来消瘦
他咬着子弹，探向内心
寻找尊严

有人给我看一张照片，我只是笑
尊严从未被拍摄到

I went into the red, went into the black
Into the valley of dry bone dreams

So many roads, so much at stake
So many dead ends, I'm at the edge of the lake
Sometimes I wonder what it's gonna take
To find dignity

我弄出了赤字，弄出了黑字[1]
进入枯骨梦境的山谷

这么多的路，这么多的风险
这么多的死胡同，我在湖水边
有时我好奇，究竟要付出什么
才能找到尊严

[1] “赤字”指亏损，“黑字”指盈利。这句话的意思是负过债，赚过钱。

# *UNDER THE RED SKY*
# 红色天空下

扭扭摆摆

红色天空下

难以置信

生逢其时

关于电视话题的歌

10000 个男人

2 × 2

上帝知道

猜手手公子

猫在井下

handy dandy

1/ handy dandy contrversy always surrounds him
wherefer he goes too bad for him ~~something back there always hounds him~~

2. handy dandy he ~~was~~ in a room all ~~just~~ pacing the floor that supports him
in better times anyghing he desired would have just kept walking on
pushing towrd towrds him
of power power his respectability dont bother
covering

3. handy dandy a tower of strenght & stability
he does it with mirrors but he doesnt really, do actually
he dont need to lie cause he's so full of humility
acceseessable

2handy da, compulsive & healty, plausible obsesive automatic
bloin g his horn for the girls & ~~bringing~~ them up tothe attic
for the girl ~~[illegible]~~ running them up

5. handy..... will well yeal mayble
he ~~xxxxx~~ how much do you weigh

6. he's in a rom full ov people and somuddeny theres nobody cheering
~~itxsinkxxhexxtxhi~~he says c'mon baby lets both take the wheel to this
car it dont matter~~xxxxxx~~ who is steering

迪伦的《红色天空下》发行于1990年9月10日，该创作的部分起因或可归于他的女儿。专辑题献给“加比咕咕”（Gabby Goo Goo），直到2001年人们才明白，“加比咕咕”是迪伦的小女儿，时年4岁。当时，迪伦与卡罗琳·丹尼斯的婚姻处于完全秘密的状态，不为公众知晓。

这是迪伦第27张录音室专辑。前一年，他刚出版了广受好评的专辑《哦，慈悲》。绝大多数评论家难掩对新专辑的失望。迪伦自己也承认制作不佳，只差直接说出来——制作所托非人。

这张专辑的制作交给了唐·沃斯和戴维·沃斯（Don & David Was），迪伦化名参与了联合制作。这哥俩都是新崛起的英国优秀音乐人，可惜制作经验不足。出于对之前制作人丹尼尔·拉努瓦苛刻作风的厌烦，也是想换个方向，迪伦这次在制作上基本上“甩手”，不操心不细心不用心。

要说这3位，在音乐创作的理念上其实是蛮默契的，彼此高度认同。他们从不交流想法，迪伦从不提前给哥俩听他要录的歌，这哥俩也从不提前告诉迪伦会有哪些乐手参与录制。每次迪伦走进录音室——哟嗬！都是熟人啊，都是名人啊。

可能双方都把问题想简单了。迪伦想的是，这是一辑“伪童谣”，需要沃斯哥俩那种简洁而兴致盎然的乐声。而沃斯哥俩想的是，每场录音都请来最好的乐手、不同的乐手，凭这些天才的才华，制作不可能不好。

然而，这是迪伦多年来，我估算，是至少 8 年来的完整创作。这种处心积虑、构思完整的创作，起码要回溯到“基督教三部曲”时期，才能找到。就算是那个时期的作品，也达不到这张专辑的整体水平。它是需要通盘筹划的，即兴的碰撞成就不了大业。

结果就是，尽管众星云集，乔治·哈里森（George Harrison）、戴维·克罗斯比（David Crosby）、埃尔顿·约翰（Elton John）、布鲁斯·霍恩斯比（Bruce Hornsby）、阿尔·库珀、斯莱什（Slash）、史蒂维·雷·沃恩和吉米·沃恩（Stevie Ray & Jimmie Vaughan）……却无助于为该专辑塑形，给予这些“伪童谣”真正的神魂。

就只说歌词吧，《红色天空下》是一辑真正的杰作，以诗歌观念来说，它是一辑组诗，是一部诗集。

歌词中有大量对英语童谣的引用和摹写，又有诸多对《圣经》素材的移用、改写和变形。通观前后，则有一种整体性。各首歌词之间存在着若有若无、或强或弱的呼应和关联；整部专辑一以贯之，似是对人类命运的关切与忧虑，有着预言和启示录的色彩。

与以前的作品比起来，迪伦这回完全收起了他备受瞩目的做派，改变了形象。滔滔不绝不见了，文字简净乃至干枯。汪洋恣肆、瑰丽斑斓、天马行空不见了，暴风骤雨顿歇，烈马收住了缰绳。童谣的结构乃至用语、修辞占据主导，但总体的印象却苍老、肃静、沉重。循环的节奏和韵律，极简呈冷色调的意象和形象，神秘的人物和情节，具有神圣色彩的警诫和宗教谕示，都通过童谣体予以凸显，并取得艺术性的平衡。

这张专辑还有一个特点就是游戏性。游戏性不仅是这些词作的美学特征，也是诸多篇目的灵感来源和推动力，使得一种近似童话、神话或寓言、谜语的诗境，在游戏中出现并连绵展开，活泼而兴奋。其中，既有天真未知、兴高采烈的欢乐和玩闹，也有置身事外、不动声色，仿似天地不仁的静观和呈示。相较于歌词，其音乐方面都不舒展，有时枯瘦寡淡。迪伦此前感染力强烈的咆哮与哀鸣，也荡然无存。

许多音乐批评者对此完全无感，因此，开篇曲《扭扭摆摆》，终于出现在“迪伦最差歌曲”的选单上。但就算是这首歌，也是杰作，那是不求意义地回归于形式，认识到童谣中有最天真的欢笑、最欢快的舞蹈。

该专辑的具体录音信息难以确认。大致看，主要是在加州洛杉矶和好莱坞的四五家录音室，靠近迪伦在马里布的家，从 1990 年 1 月 6 日至 5 月 25 日，进行了多场录音和 10 多场叠录。

迪伦传记透露，该专辑令人失望的销量让迪伦郁闷不已。更糟的是，第二任妻子卡罗琳，在 1990 年 8 月该专辑出版前，与迪伦签署了离婚协议。

## WIGGLE WIGGLE

Wiggle, wiggle, wiggle like a gypsy queen
Wiggle, wiggle, wiggle all dressed in green
Wiggle, wiggle, wiggle 'til the moon is blue
Wiggle 'til the moon sees you

Wiggle, wiggle, wiggle in your boots and shoes
Wiggle, wiggle, wiggle, you got nothing to lose
Wiggle, wiggle, wiggle like a swarm of bees
Wiggle on your hands and knees

Wiggle to the front, wiggle to the rear
Wiggle 'til you wiggle right out of here
Wiggle 'til it opens, wiggle 'til it shuts
Wiggle 'til it bites, wiggle 'til it cuts

Wiggle, wiggle, wiggle like a bowl of soup
Wiggle, wiggle, wiggle like a rolling hoop
Wiggle, wiggle, wiggle like a ton of lead
Wiggle—you can raise the dead

# 扭扭摆摆 [1]

扭扭摆摆扭扭摆摆像吉卜赛女王
扭扭摆摆扭扭摆摆上上下下着绿装
扭扭摆摆扭扭摆摆直到月亮变成蓝色
扭扭摆摆直到月亮看见你

扭扭摆摆扭扭摆摆随你的靴你的鞋
扭扭摆摆扭扭摆摆没什么会失去
扭扭摆摆扭扭摆摆像一群蜜蜂
扭扭摆摆用你的手和你的膝

扭摆到前，扭摆到后
扭摆直到你扭摆出了这里
扭摆直到它开，扭摆直到它关
扭摆直到它咬，扭摆直到它断

扭扭摆摆扭扭摆摆像一碗汤
扭扭摆摆扭扭摆摆像一个滚环
扭扭摆摆扭扭摆摆像一吨铅
扭扭摆摆——你能使死者复活

---

[1] 这一辑全部由郝佳校译。

Wiggle 'til you're high, wiggle 'til you're higher
Wiggle 'til you vomit fire
Wiggle 'til it whispers, wiggle 'til it hums
Wiggle 'til it answers, wiggle 'til it comes

Wiggle, wiggle, wiggle like satin and silk
Wiggle, wiggle, wiggle like a pail of milk
Wiggle, wiggle, wiggle, rattle and shake
Wiggle like a big fat snake

扭摆直到你高，扭摆直到你更高
扭摆直到你喷出火
扭摆直到它低语，扭摆直到它哼哼
扭摆直到它作答，扭摆直到它到来

扭扭摆摆扭扭摆摆像缎和绸
扭扭摆摆扭扭摆摆像一桶奶
扭扭摆摆扭摆、摇晃、摇出响声
扭扭摆摆像一条又肥又大的蛇

## UNDER THE RED SKY

There was a little boy and there was a little girl
And they lived in an alley under the red sky
There was a little boy and there was a little girl
And they lived in an alley under the red sky

There was an old man and he lived in the moon
One summer's day he came passing by
There was an old man and he lived in the moon
And one day he came passing by

Someday little girl, everything for you is gonna be new
Someday little girl, you'll have a diamond as big as your shoe

Let the wind blow low, let the wind blow high

## 红色天空下

有一个小男孩，有一个小女孩[1]
他们住在一条小巷在红色的天空下
有一个小男孩，有一个小女孩
他们住在一条小巷在红色的天空下

有一个老人住在月亮上[2]
夏日的一天他打此地经过
有一个老人住在月亮上
有一天他打此地经过

有一天小女孩，所有一切对你都将变成新的
有一天小女孩，你将得到像你鞋子一样大的钻石[3]

让风低低吹，让风高高吹[4]

---

[1] 19世纪初英文童谣《有一个小男孩和一个小女孩》："有一个小男孩和一个小女孩/住在一条小巷里"。"有一个小……有一个小……"是童谣常见的句式。

[2] 爱尔兰童谣《艾肯·加姆》："有个人住在月亮上，住在月亮上，住在月亮上/有个人住在月亮上/他叫艾肯·加姆。"

[3] 英文童谣："小女孩，小女孩，你去了哪里？/采玫瑰给皇后。/小女孩，小女孩，她送你什么？/她送我一颗像鞋子一样大的钻石。"

[4] 类似英美儿童游戏的开头唱句，有不同版本，如"风吹低/风吹高/星星天上掉""风，风，风吹高/雨从天上掉"。

One day the little boy and the little girl were both baked in a pie
Let the wind blow low, let the wind blow high
One day the little boy and the little girl were both baked in a pie

This is the key to the kingdom and this is the town
This is the blind horse that leads you around

Let the bird sing, let the bird fly
One day the man in the moon went home and the river went dry
Let the bird sing, let the bird fly
The man in the moon went home and the river went dry

一天小男孩和小女孩双双在一个馅饼中烤着[1]
让风低低吹，让风高高吹
一天小男孩和小女孩双双在一个馅饼中烤着

这是打开王国的钥匙，这是那小镇
这是那匹瞎马[2]它领着你乱转

让鸟儿唱，让鸟儿飞
一天月亮上的人回家了河流变得干涸
让鸟儿唱，让鸟儿飞
月亮上的人回家了河流变得干涸

---

[1] 《鹅妈妈童谣·唱一首六便士的歌》："……二十四只黑鸟 / 在馅饼中烤 // 当馅饼打开 / 鸟儿开始叫……"19 世纪英文童谣亦有"宝贝和我 / 在馅饼中烤"之句。

[2] 英文童谣有"我花十个先令买了匹老瞎马"之句。

## UNBELIEVABLE

It's unbelievable, it's strange but true
It's inconceivable it could happen to you
You go north and you go south
Just like bait in the fish's mouth
Ya must be livin' in the shadow of some kind of evil star
It's unbelievable it would get this far

It's undeniable what they'd have you to think
It's indescribable, it can drive you to drink
They said it was the land of milk and honey
Now they say it's the land of money
Who ever thought they could ever make that stick
It's unbelievable you can get this rich this quick

Every head is so dignified
Every moon is so sanctified
Every urge is so satisfied as long as you're with me
All the silver, all the gold
All the sweethearts you can hold
That don't come back with stories untold
Are hanging on a tree

# 难以置信

难以置信，这很奇怪却是真的
难以想象，这会发生在你身上
你走向北，你走向南
好像鱼嘴中的诱饵
你肯定生活在哪颗灾星的阴影中
难以置信它可以笼罩得这么远

难以否认他们让你思考的事儿
难以形容，它能驱使你狂饮
他们曾说这里是奶与蜜之地
现在则说这是金钱之地
谁承想他们说中了
难以置信你能这么快这么富裕

每一颗头颅这么庄严
每一颗月亮这么神圣
每一个冲动这么满足，只要你跟我在一起
所有的银，所有的金
所有你能拥有的情人
悬挂在一棵树上
不会在未讲的故事中重现

It's unbelievable like a lead balloon
It's so impossible to even learn the tune
Kill that beast and feed that swine
Scale that wall and smoke that vine
Feed that horse and saddle up the drum
It's unbelievable, the day would finally come

Once there was a man who had no eyes
Every lady in the land told him lies
He stood beneath the silver sky and his heart began to bleed
Every brain is civilized
Every nerve is analyzed
Everything is criticized when you are in need

It's unbelievable, it's fancy-free
So interchangeable, so delightful to see
Turn your back, wash your hands
There's always someone who understands
It don't matter no more what you got to say
It's unbelievable it would go down this way

难以置信像一只铅气球[1]
就连学那曲调都如此不可能
杀掉那畜生喂养那蠢猪
攀上那堵墙熏死那藤蔓
喂肥骏马把鼓备上鞍
难以置信，那一天终将来临

从前有个人他瞎了眼
那片土地上的每个淑女都对他说假话
他站在银色天空下，他的心开始流血
每个大脑都被开化
每根神经都被解析
每件事都被批评，在你需要帮助的时候

难以置信，无拘无束
如此轻易转换，如此赏心悦目
转过你的背，洗干净你的手
总会有人明白
你再说什么都无所谓
难以置信会继续这样下去

---

[1] 像一只铅气球（like a lead balloon），英文习语，指毫无用处。

## BORN IN TIME

In the lonely night
In the blinking stardust of a pale blue light
You're comin' thru to me in black and white
When we were made of dreams

You're blowing down the shaky street
You're hearing my heart beat
In the record-breaking heat
Where we were born in time

Not one more night, not one more kiss
Not this time baby, no more of this
Takes too much skill, takes too much will
It's revealing
You came, you saw, just like the law
You married young, just like your ma
You tried and tried, you made me slide
You left me reelin' with this feelin'

On the rising curve

## 生逢其时

孤独之夜
从闪耀着微蓝光芒的星团[1]
你在黑白中向我袭来
当我们是用梦做成的

你吹过不安的街
你倾听我的心
在破纪录的高温中
我们生逢其时

不要再多一夜，不要再多一吻
这一次不了宝贝，再不要这样
需要太多的技巧，需要太多的意志
这实在明显不过
你来了，你看到，就像是法律
你早早结婚，就像你的妈妈
你试了又试，让我滑倒
让我摆脱不了这种感觉

在上升的曲线上

---

[1] 星团（stardust），也可解作口语中的“梦幻”。

Where the ways of nature will test every nerve
You won't get anything you don't deserve
Where we were born in time

You pressed me once, you pressed me twice
You hang the flame, you'll pay the price
Oh babe, that fire
Is still smokin'
You were snow, you were rain
You were striped, you were plain
Oh babe, truer words
Have not been spoken or broken

In the hills of mystery
In the foggy web of destiny
You can have what's left of me
Where we were born in time

每根神经受到自然规律的考验
你得不到你不应得的
我们生逢其时

你逼我一次，又逼我一次
你悬置那火焰，你将付出代价
噢宝贝，那火
仍在冒烟
你是雪，你是雨
你是条纹的，你是单色的
噢宝贝，没有人说过讲过
比这更真的话

在神秘的山中
在雾蒙蒙的命运之网里
你可以得到残留的我
我们生逢其时

## T.V. TALKIN' SONG

One time in London I'd gone out for a walk
Past a place called Hyde Park where people talk
'Bout all kinds of different gods, they have their point of view
To anyone passing by, that's who they're talking to

There was someone on a platform talking to the folks
About the T.V. god and all the pain that it invokes
"It's too bright a light," he said, "for anybody's eyes
If you've never seen one it's a blessing in disguise"

I moved in closer, got up on my toes
Two men in front of me were coming to blows
The man was saying something 'bout children when they're young
Being sacrificed to it while lullabies are being sung

"The news of the day is on all the time
All the latest gossip, all the latest rhyme
Your mind is your temple, keep it beautiful and free
Don't let an egg get laid in it by something you can't see"

"Pray for peace!" he said. You could feel it in the crowd
My thoughts began to wander. His voice was ringing loud

## 关于电视话题的歌

在伦敦城有一次我出外散步
经过一个叫海德公园的地方那儿有人高谈阔论
关于各种不同的神，他们有他们的观点
每一个路人，都是他们谈话的对象

讲台上有人正在向人群演讲
关于电视神及其引起的各种痛苦
“对人的眼睛来说，”他说，“它的光太亮
如果你从没看过它，那似是遗憾，实乃幸福”

我走近前去，踮起脚尖
站我前面的两人正准备动手互殴
台上那男子正在说什么孩子很小
在摇篮曲唱起时就已沦为它的牺牲品

“每时每刻都播着今日新闻
所有最近的八卦，所有最新的歌
心是你的神殿，要让它保持美丽自由
别让你不了解的东西，把它的蛋下在里头”

“祈求平安！”他说。你能够感到人群在应和
我的思想开始漂游。他的调门提得老高

"It will destroy your family, your happy home is gone
No one can protect you from it once you turn it on"

"It will lead you into some strange pursuits
Lead you to the land of forbidden fruits
It will scramble up your head and drag your brain about
Sometimes you gotta do like Elvis did and shoot the damn thing out"

"It's all been designed," he said, "to make you lose your mind
And when you go back to find it, there's nothing there to find
Every time you look at it, your situation's worse
If you feel it grabbing out for you, send for the nurse"

The crowd began to riot and they grabbed hold of the man
There was pushing, there was shoving and everybody ran
The T.V. crew was there to film it, they jumped right over me
Later on that evening, I watched it on T.V.

“它将毁了你的家庭，你幸福的家将失去
一旦你打开它，就没人能保护你”

“它将引你进入奇怪的追逐
带你进入禁果之地
它会搅乱你的头，拖着你的脑子乱走
有时你必须像埃尔维斯[1]那样，把那该死的东西射穿”[2]

“一切都设计好了，”他说，“让人失去头脑
当你想把它找回，却已什么都找不到”
“每看一次，你的情况就变得更糟
如果你感到它在抓你，赶紧去叫护士”

人群开始骚动，有人冲过去抓住那男人
大家前推后搡，每个人都在跑
电视摄制组在那儿录像，他们跃过我
当天晚上稍晚，我在电视里看到了这报道

---

[1] 埃尔维斯，此处指“猫王”，摇滚乐历史上第一个偶像。

[2] 有报道说，有一次“猫王”看电视，电视中不知什么引起了他的不快，“猫王”拿起手枪将电视机击碎。

## 10,000 MEN

Ten thousand men on a hill
Ten thousand men on a hill
Some of 'm goin' down, some of 'm gonna get killed

Ten thousand men dressed in oxford blue
Ten thousand men dressed in oxford blue
Drummin' in the morning, in the evening they'll be coming for you

Ten thousand men on the move
Ten thousand men on the move
None of them doing nothin' that your mama wouldn't disapprove

Ten thousand men digging for silver and gold
Ten thousand men digging for silver and gold
All clean shaven, all coming in from the cold

Hey! Who could your lover be?
Hey! Who could your lover be?

## 10000 个男人

一万个男人在山上
一万个男人在山上
他们中一些人走下来，一些人将被杀害

一万个男人身穿牛津蓝[1]
一万个男人身穿牛津蓝
在早晨击鼓，在傍晚向你扑来

一万个男人在行进
一万个男人在行进
他们中没人做你妈妈不同意的事情

一万个男人挖金掘银
一万个男人挖金掘银
所有人脸刮得干净，所有人不再受冷清

嘿！哪个会是你的爱人？
嘿！哪个会是你的爱人？

---

[1] 牛津蓝，一种深蓝中带紫的颜色。

Let me eat off his head so you can really see!

Ten thousand women all dressed in white
Ten thousand women all dressed in white
Standin' at my window wishing me goodnight

Ten thousand men looking so lean and frail
Ten thousand men looking so lean and frail
Each one of 'm got seven wives, each one of 'm just out of jail

Ten thousand women all sweepin' my room
Ten thousand women all sweepin' my room
Spilling my buttermilk, sweeping it up with a broom

Ooh, baby, thank you for my tea!
Baby, thank you for my tea!
It's so sweet of you to be so nice to me

让我吃掉他的头[1]，这样你好真的看清！

一万个女人一身白衣
一万个女人一身白衣
站在我的窗前，祝我晚安

一万个男人又瘦又弱
一万个男人又瘦又弱
每一个人娶了七个老婆，每一个人都刚刚出狱

一万个女人打扫着我的房
一万个女人打扫着我的房
打翻了我的酪乳，用扫帚清理掉

噢宝贝，谢谢你的茶！
宝贝，谢谢你的茶！
你是多么甜，对我多么好

[1] 英文童谣《一只长尾猪》："抓住它的尾巴，/ 再吃掉它的头，/ 你才能够放心 / 这猪公已死透。"这里指做成猪形状的糕点。

## 2 × 2

One by one, they followed the sun
One by one, until there were none
Two by two, to their lovers they flew
Two by two, into the foggy dew
Three by three, they danced on the sea
Four by four, they danced on the shore
Five by five, they tried to survive
Six by six, they were playing with tricks

How many paths did they try and fail?
How many of their brothers and sisters lingered in jail?
How much poison did they inhale?
How many black cats crossed their trail?

Seven by seven, they headed for heaven
Eight by eight, they got to the gate
Nine by nine, they drank the wine
Ten by ten, they drank it again

## 2 × 2 [1]

一跟一，他们去追日
一跟一，直到都消逝
二跟二，飞去会情侣
二跟二，进入雾中露 [2]
三跟三，他们海上舞
四跟四，他们岸边舞
五跟五，他们要活命
六跟六，他们要把戏

有多少路试过未成？
有多少兄弟姐妹苟活狱中？
有多少毒气被吸进？
有多少黑猫穿过小径？

七跟七，他们天堂去
八跟八，他们到门口
九跟九，他们喝酒
十跟十，他们再喝

---

[1] 歌词中的关键词“by”，是数学中的“乘以”，又是“跟着”的意思，一语双关。

[2] 雾中露，是数首歌的歌名，其中至少有 3 首属于凯尔特民歌。

How many tomorrows have they given away?
How many compared to yesterday?
How many more without any reward?
How many more can they afford?

Two by two, they stepped into the ark
Two by two, they step in the dark
Three by three, they're turning the key
Four by four, they turn it some more

One by one, they follow the sun
Two by two, to another rendezvous

有多少明日被虚掷？

有多少明日比昨日？

还有多少明日无酬劳？

还有多少明日可挥斥？

二跟二，他们进方舟

二跟二，他们入黑暗

三跟三，他们转钥匙

四跟四，他们再转

一跟一，他们去追日

二跟二，去下个约会地

## GOD KNOWS

God knows you ain't pretty
God knows it's true
God knows there ain't anybody
Ever gonna take the place of you

God knows it's a struggle
God knows it's a crime
God knows there's gonna be no more water
But fire next time

God don't call it treason
God don't call it wrong
It was supposed to last a season
But it's been so strong for so long

God knows it's fragile
God knows everything
God knows it could snap apart right now
Just like putting scissors to a string

God knows it's terrifying
God sees it all unfold

## 上帝知道

上帝知道你不美
上帝知道这是真的
上帝知道没有人
要取代你

上帝知道这是斗争
上帝知道这是犯罪
上帝知道不会再是水了
下一回会是火

上帝不叫它背叛
上帝不叫它犯错
它本该再延续一季
可它坚挺了这么久

上帝知道这脆弱
上帝知道一切
上帝知道随时会断成两截
就像绳子遇上剪子

上帝知道这可怖
上帝看见一切崭露

There's a million reasons for you to be crying
You been so bold and so cold

God knows that when you see it
God knows you've got to weep
God knows the secrets of your heart
He'll tell them to you when you're asleep

God knows there's a river
God knows how to make it flow
God knows you ain't gonna be taking
Nothing with you when you go

God knows there's a purpose
God knows there's a chance
God knows you can rise above the darkest hour
Of any circumstance

God knows there's a heaven
God knows it's out of sight
God knows we can get all the way from here to there
Even if we've got to walk a million miles by candlelight

你有一百万个理由哭
你一直如此大胆又如此冷酷

上帝知道当你看到它
上帝知道你定会哭泣
上帝知道你心里那些秘密
在你睡着时他会将秘密告诉你

上帝知道有条河
上帝知道如何让它流
上帝知道你什么都带不走
在你离去的时候

上帝知道有个目的
上帝知道有次机会
上帝知道你能熬过最黑暗时刻
在任何情况下

上帝知道有个天堂
上帝知道它看不见
上帝知道我们能从这走到那
就算秉着烛光走一百万英里

## HANDY DANDY

Handy Dandy, controversy surrounds him
He been around the world and back again
Something in the moonlight still hounds him
Handy Dandy, just like sugar and candy

Handy Dandy, if every bone in his body was broken he would never admit it
He got an all-girl orchestra and when he says
"Strike up the band," they hit it
Handy Dandy, Handy Dandy

You say, "What are ya made of?"
He says, "Can you repeat what you said?"
You'll say, "What are you afraid of?"
He'll say, "Nothin'! Neither 'live nor dead."

## 猜手手公子[1]

猜手手公子，周围全是争议
他环游了世界，又回来
月光中有什么还在追逐他
猜手手公子，就像糖块与糖果

猜手手公子，就算他的每一根骨头都折了，
　他也不会承认
他有一个全女子管弦乐队，当他说
“开始演奏”，她们就演奏
猜手手公子，猜手手公子

你说：“你是用什么做的？[2]”
他说：“你能重复一遍问题吗？”
你会说：“什么是你惧怕的？”
他会说：“没有！无论生还是死。[3]”

---

[1] handy dandy，儿童游戏，一人双手成拳，让别人猜哪只手里攥有小物件。猜前双拳快速上下互绕，念“猜手手公子哥儿 / 甜腻腻的糖果儿 / 在上头？在下头？ / 猜手手儿了不得 / 小小的公子哥儿 / 你猜猜藏在哪只手儿”。

[2] 英文童谣中有“小男孩和小女孩是用什么做的”之语。

[3] 童话《杰克与魔豆》中的巨人有“管他活着还是死了 / 我要碾他的骨头做面包”之语。

Handy Dandy, he got a stick in his hand and a pocket full of
money
He says, "Darling, tell me the truth, how much time I got?"
She says, "You got all the time in the world, honey"
Handy Dandy, Handy Dandy

He's got that clear crystal fountain
He's got that soft silky skin
He's got that fortress on the mountain
With no doors, no windows, no thieves can break in

Handy Dandy, sitting with a girl named Nancy in a garden
feelin' kind of lazy
He says, "Ya want a gun? I'll give ya one." She says, "Boy, you
talking crazy"
Handy Dandy, just like sugar and candy
Handy Dandy, pour him another brandy

Handy Dandy, he got a basket of flowers and a bag full of

猜手手公子，他手里抓着拐杖，口袋里
　装满钱[1]
他说："亲爱的，告诉我实情，我有多少时间？"
她说："你有世界上所有的时间，亲爱的"
猜手手公子，猜手手公子

他有水晶般清澈的喷泉
他有丝绸般柔软的皮肤[2]
他有山顶的城堡
没有门，没有窗，没有贼人能闯入

猜手手公子，跟一个叫南希的女孩，
　懒洋洋坐在花园里
他说："你要支枪吗？我给你。"
　她说："天哪，你疯了吗"
猜手手公子，就像糖块与糖果
猜手手公子，再给他倒杯白兰地

猜手手公子，他得到一篮子花和一袋子

---

[1] "……他手里抓着拐杖 / 喉咙有颗石子 / 你若给我解谜 / 我就给你银币。"谜底是樱桃或山楂果。

[2] "他有水晶般清澈的喷泉 / 他有丝绸般柔软的皮肤"，改写自一则谜语："大理石墙白如乳 / 衬入丝绸般柔肤 / 中有晶澈之喷泉 / 金苹果于其间现 / 无门可通此要塞 / 贼人偏闯窃金来。"谜底是鸡蛋。

sorrow

He finishes his drink, he gets up from the table, he says

"Okay, boys, I'll see you tomorrow"

Handy Dandy, Handy Dandy, just like sugar and candy

Handy Dandy, just like sugar and candy

忧伤[1]

他喝光杯中酒，从桌子边站起来，说
“好了，孩子们，咱们明天见”
猜手手公子，猜手手公子，就像糖块与糖果
猜手手公子，就像糖块与糖果

[1] 一篮子花，英文童谣云：“床上有只篮子 / 篮子里有些花儿……”。

## CAT'S IN THE WELL

The cat's in the well, the wolf is looking down
The cat's in the well, the wolf is looking down
He got his big bushy tail dragging all over the ground

The cat's in the well, the gentle lady is asleep
Cat's in the well, the gentle lady is asleep
She ain't hearing a thing, the silence is a-stickin' her deep

The cat's in the well and grief is showing its face
The world's being slaughtered and it's such a bloody disgrace

The cat's in the well, the horse is going bumpety bump
The cat's in the well, and the horse is going bumpety bump
Back alley Sally is doing the American jump

The cat's in the well, and Papa is reading the news
His hair's falling out and all of his daughters need shoes

The cat's in the well and the barn is full of bull
The cat's in the well and the barn is full of bull

## 猫在井下

猫在井下，狼在上面看着
猫在井下，狼在上面看着
他毛蓬蓬的大尾巴满地拖

猫在井下，温柔的女士睡了
猫在井下，温柔的女士睡了
她什么也听不见，寂静包围着她

猫在井下，悲伤露出它的脸
世界正被屠戮，这是怎样一个该死的耻辱

猫在井下，马儿颠颠儿跑
猫在井下，马儿颠颠儿跑
后巷里的莎莉在玩“美国跳”[1]

猫在井下，爸爸在读新闻
他的头发在脱落，他的女儿们都需要鞋

猫在井下，栏里满是公牛
猫在井下，栏里满是公牛

---

[1] 美国跳，大人抓着小孩的手蹦跳的游戏。

The night is so long and the table is oh, so full

The cat's in the well and the servant is at the door
The drinks are ready and the dogs are going to war

The cat's in the well, the leaves are starting to fall
The cat's in the well, leaves are starting to fall
Goodnight, my love, may the Lord have mercy on us all

夜这样长，桌子啊这样满

猫在井下，仆人在门口
酒准备好了，狗[1]将投入战斗

猫在井下，树叶开始落了
猫在井下，树叶开始落了
晚安，我的爱，愿主垂怜我们

[1] 狗（dog），在口语中也有“男人、小伙子”之意。